Fly Fishing on

For additional copies contact:

bwillmert@suddenlink.net

or

mordekai38@gmail.com

1/21/2015
To Patrick,
I hope to see
you on the river,
Best Fishes,
B Willmert

Fly Fishing on the Red

Copyright © 2007, 2008, 2009, 2010

Bill Willmert

COPYRIGHT NOTICE:

Fly Fishing on the Red is copyrighted © 2007, 2008, 2009, 2010 by Bill Willmert and John Smith. All rights reserved. No part of this book may be reproduced in any form by any electronic or mechanical means (including photocopying, recording, or information storage and retrieval) without permission in writing from the copyright holder. On occasion, excerpts may be used as quotes or supporting information in other written text. These are explicitly attributed under 'fair use' provisions. All photos used with permission. For all permissions, please contact the author at bwillert@suddenlink.net.

DISCLAIMER:

This is not a work of fiction. However, any similarity to any person living or dead, other than explicitly named interview subjects, is purely coincidental. Many portions of this publication offer advice, tips and techniques to help a struggling angler catch bigger fish. That being said, the projections, trends, forecasts, and conclusions provided herein should not be construed as being definitive. These techniques appear to work for the fishermen who currently use them. No assurances are offered, either implicitly or explicitly, that these techniques, tips, tricks, etc, will work for everyone or anyone. All this being said, this book is a true reflection of the individuals interviewed.

Dedication:

To the late Jimmy Stewart

Who taught me not to take a minute of time on the water for granted and who was one of the true gentlemen of the river.

To the late Captain John Zwicky

Who taught me that the best lessons of all were learned on the water with friends and that some of life's best catches are caught under dark skies.

Table of Contents:

Forward	5
Introduction	6
Area Map	8
Heber Springs	10
Why the Little Red?	11

Interviews:	**Page**
Denise Barton	12
Frank Barton	20
Tom Bly	28
Bob Cotten	38
Chuck Farneth	47
Duane Hada	58
Jeff Hawthorne	67
Tom Hawthorne	76
Donnie Hyslip	84
Jack Kirby	91
Phil Landry	98
Rick Rasnick	105
Jamie Rouse	115
Bob Silzer	124
Ben Wiedower	133
Bill Willmert	141
Bibliography	*152*

Forward:

By John P. Smith

"I am not a fisherman; I'm a computer programmer!" I yelled that like an over-exuberant actor playing the Elephant Man when Bill Willmert first approached me with this project. How could I possibly be in any way involved in a project on fly fishing?

I didn't know anything about it, other than, it's typically the kind of fishing blue bloods do on TV. Which, of course, sparked my interest. I've always been curious about the mysterious art of fly fishing. What's the big deal? What's the allure? The appeal?

Now, I understand. It's an affliction, and an addiction and a predisposition to catch bigger, better fish. It's exactly the kind of sport that attracts hardcore individualists; people who prefer to do their own thing, find their own way, and figure it out for themselves.

So, in putting this work together, we ended up with a collection of fishing advice from a wide spectrum of individuals—from a neurologist to an eclectic artist—who gathered their data in every way imaginable. From trial and error to the scientific method to naturalistic observation, these self-motivated, self-taught experts each found a way that works for them. It's all right here in these pages.

They're not giving up secrets—they're passing on free information that is available to anyone who'll take the time to glean it from the water. They have already blazed the trail. Granted, it has many twists, turns and branches, but the beauty of it is that it always terminates on the end of a fly fishing line in the waters of the Little Red River.

Special Thanks:

Geri Hausler for picking up the pieces when the editing and proofreading tasks started falling off the screen.

Dr. Sophie Bradford for her guidance in the areas of readability and flow.

Teri Smith for typing when it was pure drudgery.

Introduction: On The Red

Often when I am fishing our river, I see fishermen that can cast adequately and have all of the gear and gadgets that anyone could want, and yet still struggle to catch fish. Other times I see fishermen with mismatched tackle or poor casting that needs work. I think that good casting is important. I think quality equipment is a pleasure to use.

The real reason for not catching fish is a lack of knowledge. A lack of knowledge about rigging, fly selection, how seasonal and daily changes affect fishing, what water holds fish, and what equipment to use limits the catches of the Red River's guests.

Most people don't know how or where to find the information that they need. Checking with local fly shops or hiring a guide are good starts. But for the independent fisherman, time on the water and the empirical approach, may take more time than there is available.

In an effort to shorten the learning curve, I have interviewed some of rivers best, most knowledgeable and seasoned fishermen that I know. Some of these fishermen are guides, or have been successful guides; others have mastered their craft by spending hundreds of days on the river for years refining their techniques. All of these men and women have mastered the fundamentals, but differ in terms of their preferences and style.

Study the interviews. You will discover how to rig your rod for the style of fishing that you intend to do. You will learn how to select the right type of fly for the water you want to fish. You will learn what kinds of water hold fish during different times of year and throughout the day.

Please join me in the pages that follow for a conversation with some of the best fly fishermen "On the Red".

Bill Willmert

July 2009

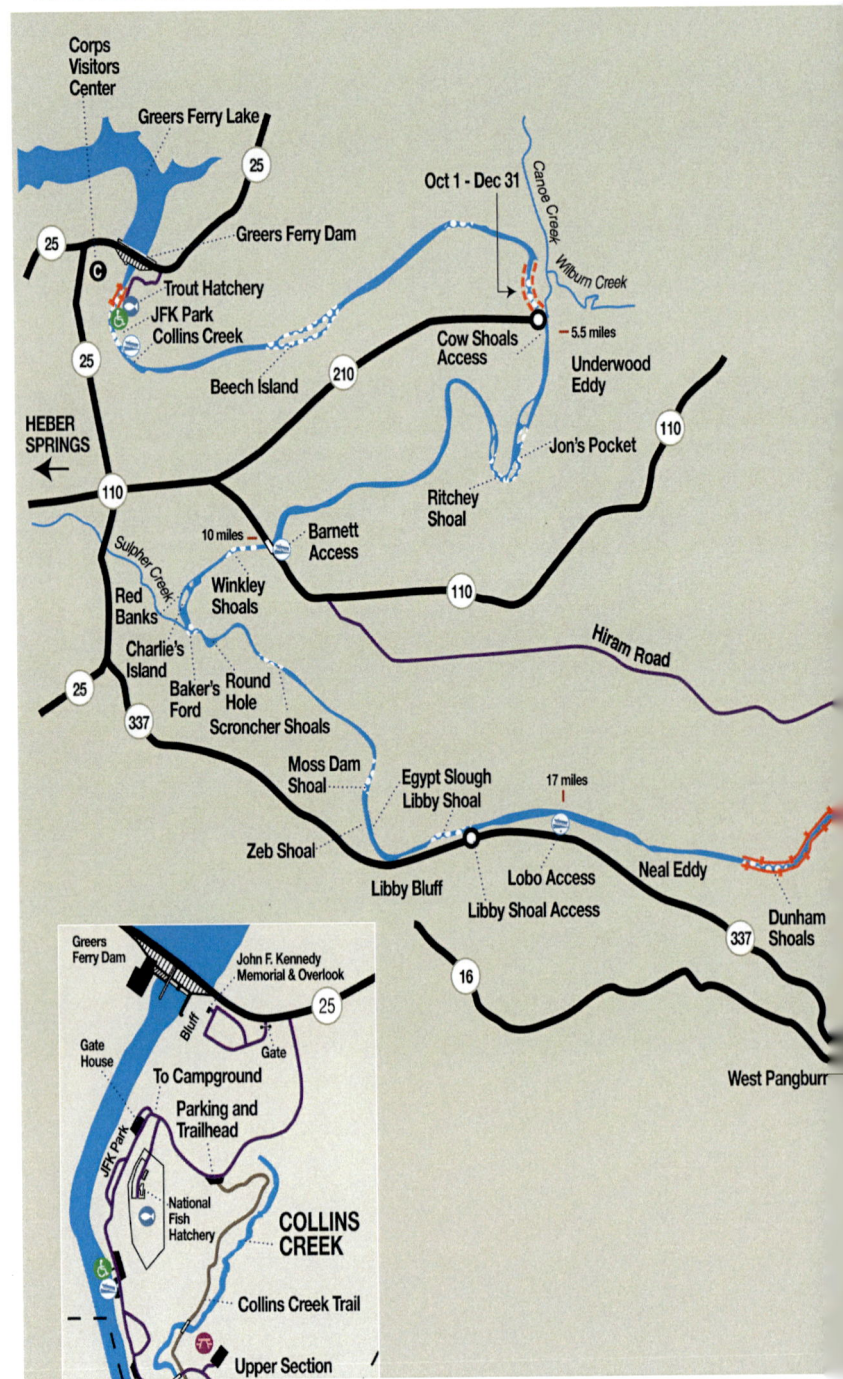

| Fly Fishing on the Red | 9 |

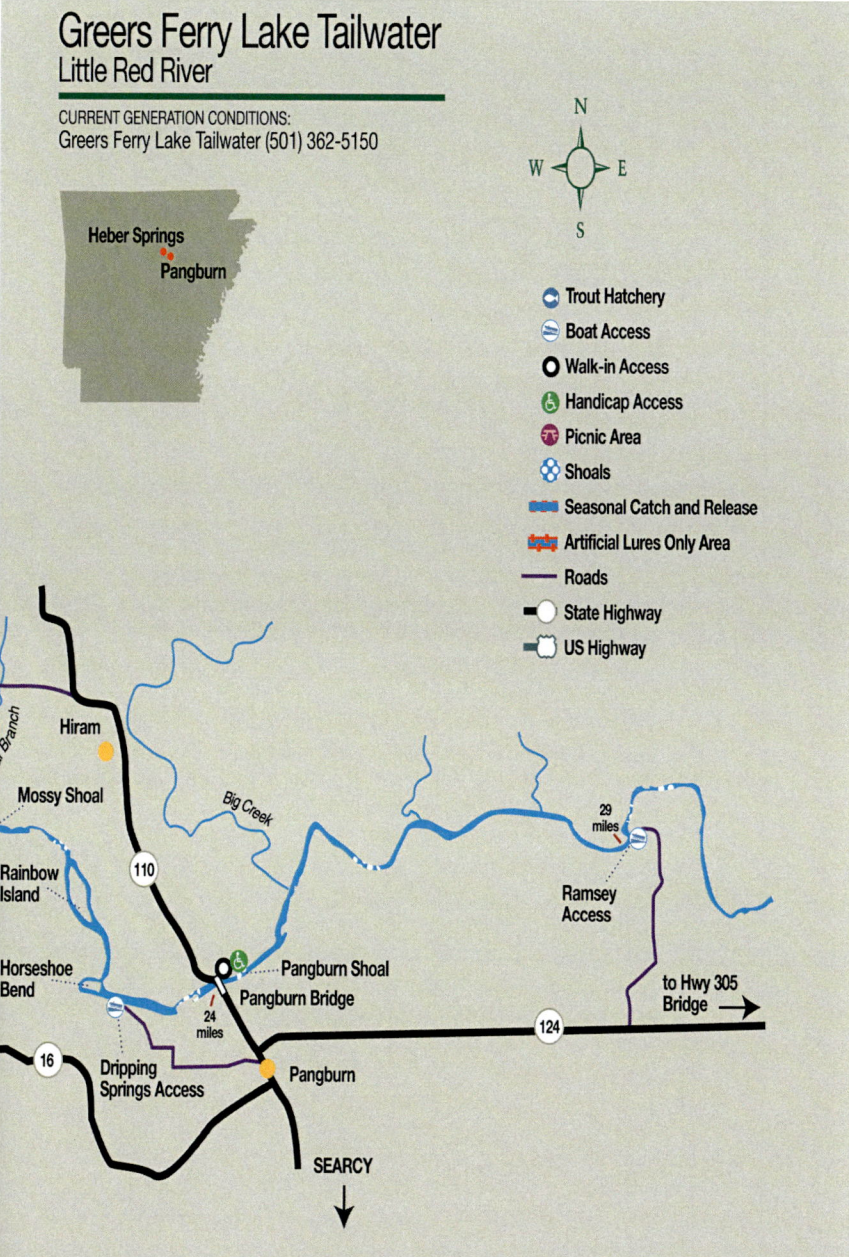

Heber Springs and Cleburne County

Heber Springs is the county seat for Cleburne County, Arkansas.

Cleburne is the state's youngest county, created in 1883 from parts of Van Buren, White and Independence counties. The people of the county are down-home, independent hearty folk whose ancestors worked the land and wrested a living through hard work and dedication to family.

Cleburne county features generally rugged terrain and elevations that range from just above sea level to as high as 1,400 feet. With plenty of water and good land, farming was the occupation of choice for most county residents in the late 19th and early 20th centuries. Early on, cotton was the big money crop along with timber cutting and logging.

The completion of the dam and reservoir in 1962 changed the face of this town and county. Business and small industry expanded with the filling of the reservoir, mostly catering to the growing tourist and vacationer trade as visitors and summer residents flocked to the area for the fishing, lake activities and camping in the hospitable climate of central Arkansas.

As for the town itself, the original settlement was known as Sugar Loaf and it was not until 1910 that the Heber Post Office was changed to Heber Springs Post Office and the town of Sugar Loaf was officially changed to Heber Springs.

Why the Red?

The Little Red River and Greers Ferry Lake are Arkansas tourist attractions. But they are not for your run-of-the-mill tourist. Unlike Six Flags, Disneyland and Silver Dollar City, the lake and river are for the tourist willing to make his own entertainment rather than settle for prefabricated fairy tale lands.

Camping, boating, floating, canoeing, rock-climbing, hiking and even scuba diving can be found in the resorts and parks surrounding the lake.

The big ticket item, however, the activity intentionally left off the previous list, is of course, fishing. The lake and Little Red River offer a world-class fishing experience for those willing to put a little work into their play. In this case, "world class" isn't just a sales pitch, either.

Greers Ferry Lake holds world records for Walleye (22 lb 11oz) and Hybrid Stripped Bass (27 lb 5 oz). The Little Red River tail water, which feeds from Greers Ferry Lake, until recently held the world-record for German Brown Trout (40 lb 4 oz.) The Little Red River is also supports a thriving Rainbow trout fishery.

Trout tend to get most of the publicity on the Little Red, but they're not the only fish in the river. Anglers could go after healthy populations of chain pickerel, spotted and smallmouth bass, green and longear sunfish, rock bass and bluegill.

Nonetheless, it's the trout fishing that the area is most known for: Trout are THE reason to fish the Little Red River. Hundreds of thousands of rainbow trout are stocked annually.

The lower Little Red River flows from the base of Greers Ferry Dam at Heber Springs to merge with the White River at the Hurricane Lake Wildlife Management Area.

Denise Barton

I commonly downsize effective saltwater patterns and adapt them for fresh water.

Denise Barton has been involved with every aspect of fly fishing for trout on the Little Red River for the past 30 years. Denise fished with and learned from some of the sport's true masters, including Dave Whitlock and Duane Hada. (Duane Hada is also featured in this publication.)

She has worked as a guide on the Little Red and also trained guides for Cutthroat Outfitters, a fly-fishing shop she co-owned and managed with her husband, Frank.

It is impossible not to be impressed with her in-depth knowledge of the river and her commitment to the fishery. To be successful year after year in a business that is generally considered a man's world is a testament to her skill and savvy.

Denise retired from guiding but still fishes the Little Red River frequently, and remains active teaching through her involvement in Casting for Recovery -- a group that teaches fly fishing to women recovering from cancer.

Interview:

Q: How long have you fished the Red River?
A: I have fished the little Red River for 30 years and worked as a guide here for 15 years.

Q: How long have you trout fished?
A: 30 years.

Q: What do you do in your non-fishing life?
A: I'm involved in real estate now. I also like to bird hunt, primarily for ducks and ruffed grouse.

Q: Have you fly fished for other fish than trout?
A: I enjoy saltwater fly fishing and have fished for redfish, permit, snook, stripers, specks, blues and salmon. I also like to fish for smallmouths.

Q: How has this influenced your trout fishing?

A: Saltwater fishing has opened my thinking in terms of patterns and techniques. I commonly downsize effective saltwater patterns and adapt them for fresh water.

Q: What do you look for in selecting a piece of water to fish?
A: I look for fish signs, for example rising fish. I like to fish cover and I'm especially fond of fishing the heads of pools.

Q: Who has influenced your fishing and how?
A: My dad got me started. He taught me to be patient. My husband Frank encouraged me to guide. (Frank Barton is also featured in this publication.) Dave Whitlock taught me to approach fishing scientifically and to study entomology. He also taught me the importance of having confidence in your techniques and patterns as well as the importance of a heightened awareness while fishing.

Q: Do you primarily wade or boat fish?
A: I prefer wading.

Q: Do you use a wading staff?
A: No.

Q: What times of day do you primarily fish?
A: My favorite time of day is 8 to 9 a.m. and then again from 3 to 5 p.m. or until dark. I consider noon an off time to fish.

Q: Do you fish high water?
A: I'll fly fish one unit of water, but not on two. When I fish high water, I'll concentrate where streams or creeks come into the river and on eddy lines.

Q: What are your favorite flies?
A: Three of my favorite patterns are zebra midges, WD-40's, and Partridge and Oranges. I also like Larva Lace bead head midges from Size 16 to 22.

Q: How do you fish them?
A: I'll dead drift most often.

Q: Does fly color matter?
A: I think so. I usually fish lighter flies in clear water.

Q: Do you use any special leaders or rigs for your favorite flies?
A: I'll normally fish a 10- to 15-foot leader. The clearer the water or the brighter the light the more important a longer leader becomes.

Q: Does your leader change with different flies?
A: I like to use a 10-foot leader for streamers when I fish from a boat. The butt of the leader has 2 feet of red 20-pound Amnesia connected to 2 feet of yellow 20-pound Amnesia. The tippet is either 4x or 5x fluorocarbon. When I midge fish, I almost always use a dropper.

Q: Do you use fluorocarbon?
A: I almost always use fluorocarbon for the last piece of tippet. To avoid problems in knot strength connecting the fluorocarbon to the monofilament, I use Duncan "Loops" for the line-to-line connection.

Q: Do you use strike indicators? What kind?
A: I use them from time to time when I fish. I'll use them a lot when I'm guiding.

Q: What size fly do you fish most often?
A: Size 16 and 18.

Q: What kind of knots do you use.
A: I tie a Duncan loop to connect the fly to the tippet. To connect the tippet to the leader I use a Duncan knot and a nail knot to connect the leader to the fly line.

Q: What is your favorite piece of equipment?
A: Easy question. I love my 4-weight Sage SLT. It's just a great rod.

Q: What tips or advice would you give a first time fisherman on the Red River?
A: Visit a local fly shop for current river conditions and patterns.

Q: What's your favorite rod, reel and line combination?
A: Again, I like a Sage 4-weight SLT with a Sage 3200 reel and Rio 4-weight Classic line.

Q: Do you tie your own flies?
A: Yes.

Q: Do you design your own flies?
A: I do; I normally modify existing patterns.

Q: What about bead heads?
A: I use them. They're OK. I like them for their weight more than anything else.

Q: How do the seasons affect your fishing?
A: I don't like to fish for spawning fish, so I don't target browns in the fall. I love to midge fish in the winter and the spring. I really like to fish early caddis hatches in the early spring.

Q: Does your fly selection change with water type or seasonally?
A: (Same as above.)

Q: Does your favorite river access change with the seasons?
A: No, I think that my favorite parts of the river are the lower stretches.

Q: How does the time of day affect your fishing?
A: I think that noon is really an off time to fish the river.

Q: Do you prefer rising, falling or stable water?
A: I like rising or stable water levels the best.

Fly Fishing on the Red

Q: Are fish signs important to your style of fishing?
A: Not that important really. If you are familiar with the water you can fish the water, and I know the water well.

Q: What is your favorite fishing technique? (Swing, strip or dead drift.)
A: Dead drifting is my favorite technique.

Q: What has been the biggest change you have seen on the Little Red River?
A: The increased development of the river is the biggest change I see. It brings its own set of problems.

Q: What changes do you or don't care for?
A: I would like to see riparian areas protected. Water quality has declined with the increase in clear cutting associated with the development.

Q: Do you ever night fish?
A: I really don't care to fish much after dusk.

WD-40

Originated by Mark Engler
Tied by Bill Willmert

Hook – Tiemco 2487 Size 18 to 20
Thread – 8/0 olive
Tail - Mallard flank feather fibers
Abdomen – Tying thread
Thorax – Tan rabbit fur
Wing Case – Mallard flank feather fibers
Head – Tying thread

Partridge and Orange

Tied by Bill Willmert

Hook – Mustad 3906 Size 16
Thread – 8/0 orange
Body – Pearsall's Gossamer Silk
Thorax – Tan rabbit fur
Hackle – Partridge feather
Head – Tying thread

Frank Barton

Learn to cast. A lot of people spend a lot of money on equipment, but can't cast.

Fly Fishing on the Red

Frank Barton is a native of Arkansas and was born in Little Rock. Frank started trout fishing with his dad on the Roaring River when he was 8 years old with a Granger bamboo rod. Now, more than 50 years later, he still fishes with that same Granger.

He describes his father as a pioneer of fishing the Arkansas tailwaters for trout. Frank's grandmother attended the dedication of Greer's Ferry Dam in 1964 by President Kennedy.

In 1979, Frank started an outdoor business "Take a Hike," specializing in hiking, climbing and white water kayaking equipment. In 1989, Frank was one of the first Americans to kayak the Chuya River in Siberia. The Berlin Wall came down months earlier in that same year. One of his river guides gave him his grandfather's Stalingrad medal to take back home to America, so the medal could be kept in a country that cherished freedom.

In 1999, Frank launched Cutthroat Flyfishers, a fly shop located in his outdoor store. At it's peak, Frank's business employed 30 people at two locations. He closed the business in 2005 and is now a real estate agent. Frank still does some guiding.

Interview:

Q: How long have you fished the Red River?
A: I've fished the Little Red for 40 years.

Q: How long have you trout fished?
A: 45 years.

Q: What did you or do you do in your non-fishing life?
A: I ran an outdoor outfitting business and a fly shop.

Q: Have you fly fished for other fish than trout?
A: I've fished for tarpon, stripers, blues and redfish. I have also fished extensively in Laguna Madre, in the Gulf of Mexico. In Arkansas, I like to fish for largemouth and smallmouth bass. In September and October I fly fish for hybrids in Greer's Ferry.

Q: How has this influenced your trout fishing?
A: I developed my love for fishing streamers from saltwater fishing.

Q: What do you look for in selecting a piece of water to fish?
A: I look for current lines and seams.

Q: Who has influenced your fishing and how?
A: My dad. Dad started fly fishing for trout in the 50's and took me along and schooled me in the basics. Dad always fished bamboo. My very first rod was a Tru-Temper steel rod.

Q: Do you primarily wade or boat fish?
A: I always prefer wading. If I fish in a boat, I like small boats, canoes or kayaks.

Q: Do you use a wading staff?
A: No.

Q: What times of day do you primarily fish?
A: Trout aren't early morning people. I don't get up early to fish.

Q: Do you fish high water?
A: Yes, I'll fish a 10-foot, 7-weight with a full sink line and a big black streamer. Usually with a Size 4 or 6 fly.

Q: What are your favorite flies?
A: One of my very favorite flies is a "Bird's Nest" developed for the Truckee River by Cal Bird.

Q: Does fly color matter?
A: I'm sure that it does. If I fish a sowbug, nine out of ten times I'll pick a drab olive or grey one.

Q: Do you use any special leaders or rigs for your favorite flies?
A: Not really. Generally I'll fish a nylon 4X tapered

leader with 3- to 4-feet of fluorocarbon tippet. For streamers, I'll fish a 9-foot, 2X leader.

Q: Does your leader change with different flies?
A: Sure, for bigger flies, I'll use a shorter stouter leader. When I'm indicator fishing, I like to use a lot of droppers. For example, in the spring I'll run a sowbug under an Elk Hair Caddis.

Q: Do you use fluorocarbon?
A: Yes, almost always when I'm fishing under an indicator.

Q: Do you use strike indicators? What kind?
A: Usually, but not always. I've started fishing more without them.

Q: What size fly do you fish most often?
A: When I fish nymphs, I fish a Size 16 or 18 most of the time. One of my very favorite flies is Size 14 black Woolly Bugger that I tie.

Q: How do you fish them?
A: I'll dead drift nymphs normally. My favorite retrieve for streamers is a dead drift, interrupted by a few strips and then dead drifted again.

Q: What kind of knots do you use.
A: To tie the fly to the tippet I'll use a cinch knot. To tie the tippet to the leader I'll use a double surgeons knot or a blood knot. Even with fluorocarbon I don't have any trouble with a blood knot breaking.

Q: What is your favorite piece of equipment?
A: My 9-foot Winston IM6 4-weight rod.

Q: What tips or advice would you give a first time fisherman on the Red River?
A: Learn to cast. A lot of people spend a lot of money on equipment, but can't cast.

Q: What's your favorite rod, reel and line combination?
A: For trout I like my 9-foot, 4-weight IM6 Winston rod, an Abel #0 trout reel with a 4-weight Rio Selective trout line. For saltwater fishing I like an Orvis Helios eight weight for streamers and an Orvis Helios five weight for big trout waters.

Q: Do you tie your own flies?
A: I tie 90% of the flies that I use. I only buy flies when I'm traveling.

Q: Do you design your own flies?
A: Some, I like to copy naturals that I see. I design a lot of my saltwater flies.

Q: What about bead heads?
A: I fish a lot of bead heads.

Q: How do the seasons affect your fishing.
A: Since there is a lot of high water in the spring, much of the fishing must be done in a boat. During that time of year, I may fish more for other warm-water fish. I love to fish hot days in the summer, wading in shorts.

Q: Does your fly selection change with water type or seasonally?
A: I really like to fish the early spring caddis hatches. I like an Elk Hair Caddis for a dry fly and I fish caddis larva with just a little dubbing over three brass beads. This pattern fishes great in high water.

Q: Does your favorite river access change with the seasons?
A: No. My favorite river access is off my dock. (Close to Richey Shoal).

Q: How does the time of day affect your fishing?
A: It really doesn't change my fishing much. If what I start with doesn't work, I make a change pretty quick.

Q: Do you prefer rising, falling or stable water?
A: Rising or stable water. I like Cow Shoals with rising water. I really like to fish when the feeder creeks are running muddy.

Q: Are fish signs important to your style of fishing?
A: Not all that much. I know the river, so I tend to fish the water more than the fish.

Q: What is your favorite fishing technique? (Swing, strip or dead drift.)
A: Stripping streamers.

Q: What has been the biggest change you have seen on the Little Red River?
A: One thing that has increased is the use of jet boats. I don't like it when they're "jetting" over shallow shoals during the spawn. I also think that jet boats contribute to shoreline erosion when they are used improperly.

Q: What changes do you or don't care for?
A: Jets have opened up the river considerably. They can be destructive. They are loud. People often use them irresponsibly.

Q: Do you ever night fish?
A: Not much.

Bird's Nest

Originated by Cal Bird
Tied by Bill Willmert

Hook – Mustad 9671 Sizes 10 to 18
Thread – 8/0 olive
Weight – 10-15 wraps .020" lead wire (optional)
Tail – 6-12 Mallard flank feather fibers
Rib – Copper wire
Abdomen – Olive dubbing
Legs – Mallard flank feather fibers
Thorax – Dubbing to match body

Woolly Bugger

Originated by Russell Blessing
Tied by Bill Willmert

Hook – Mustad 9674 or any streamer hook that you like. Sizes 4 to 12
Thread – 8/0 color to match body
Rib – Gold or silver wire (optional)
Tail – Marabou. (A blood feather tip works well.)
Hackle — Schlappen
Body — Chenile
Head —Tying thread

Thomas Bly

Always fish to rising fish. They tell you where and what they're eating.

Fly Fishing on the Red

Tom Bly was born in Newfoundland at St. John's Air Base in 1956. Tom moved with his family to Arkansas in 1969 and first started fishing for trout on the Little Red in 1986.

He started working as a guide for Lindsey's Resort on 1989, and finally picked up a fly rod in 1994. Shortly afterward, Tom began to guide for The Ozark Angler.

He is a 1978 graduate of Arkansas Tech University, Russellville, with a degree as a Biologist in Fisheries and Wildlife Management. After brief stops working in Wyoming in a uranium mine and then in Dallas, Tom started work in Heber Springs as a fishery biologist in 1987.

Now Tom is a District Fisheries Supervisor for the State of Arkansas. His background as a biologist gives him a unique understanding of how the river's systems interrelate and how and why trout act the way they do. Tom understands what trout eat, where they feed, and where they hold. He still guides for The Ozark Angler as well as independently.

Interview :

Q: How long have you fished the Red River?
A: Since 1986. Let's say for 20 years.

Q: How long have you trout fished?
A: Again, for about 20 years.

Q: What did you or do you do in your non-fishing life?
A: I'm a Biologist.

Q: Have you fly fished for other fish than trout?
A: I've fly fished for quite a few freshwater fish, including smallmouth, brim, white bass, and walleye.

Q: How has this influenced your trout fishing?
A: It hasn't changed the way I trout fish, but it has made me want to fish for other fresh water fish.

Q: What do you look for in selecting a piece of water to fish?
A: Moss beds are tough to beat. I love tailouts of shoals and then seams, pockets and runs.

Q: Who has influenced your fishing and how?
A: First, Jeff Hawthorne. Then I'd say Phil Landry. Both of these guys have been really open and shared information with me. (These two fishermen are also featured in this publication.)

Q: Do you primarily wade or boat fish?
A: My first choice is to fish out of a boat.

Q: Do you use a wading staff?
A: No.

Q: What times of day do you primarily fish?
A: I prefer to fish early, starting around 7 a.m. The first hour after sun up and evening fishing are my favorite times on the water.

Q: Do you fish high water?
A: No. It's a safety thing with me. One unit is OK. I won't fish on two units.

Q: What are your favorite flies?
A: My top fly is a sowbug. I'll also fish Soft Hackles, Brassies, a Red Ass, and midge larva. A hot glue egg is hard to beat as an egg pattern. My PT Cruiser is a Pheasant Tail variation that fishes really well under an indicator. In the summer, in low water, I like to fish Blue Wings. Then I'll fish an olive bead head Larva Lace midge pupa 6-inches to a foot under an indicator.

Q: How do you fish them?
A: I normally fish them on a dead drift.

Q: Does fly color matter?
A: I think that it does. It really depends on water clarity.

In clear water I'll fish a natural color. For example a light Sow Scud dubbing.

Q: Do you use any special leaders or rigs for your favorite flies?
A: I almost always will fish a 5X, 9-foot leader with 3- to 4-feet of 5X or 6X tippet.

Q: Does your leader change with different flies?
A: No.

Q: Do you use fluorocarbon?
A: Yes.

Q: Do you use strike indicators? What kind?
A: Yes. I use a small Styrofoam ball with a rubber band core

Q: What size fly do you fish most often?
A: Size 16

Q: What kind of knots do you use?
A: For nymphs, I'll use a double surgeons knot and for streamers, a cinch knot. To connect my fly line to the backing I use a double surgeons loop knot and to connect the fly line to the leader, I use a perfection loop.

Q: What is your favorite piece of equipment?
A: Number one is my boat. Then I would pick my Ketchum Release tool. I always fish barbless hooks.

Q: What tips or advice would you give a first-time fisherman on the Red River?
A: Hire a guide. You'll learn more in one trip than fishing for a year on your own.

Q: What's your favorite rod, reel and line combination?
A: A 9-foot, 5-weight Winston II BX rod with a Battenkill Barstock reel and Orvis Wonderline weight-forward floating line.

Q: Do you tie your own flies?
A: I tie all of the flies that I and my clients fish with.

Q: Do you design your own flies?
A: Some.

(Author's note: Tom ties one of the most realistic and natural-looking sowbugs on the river.)

Q: What about beadheads?
A: I love beadheads. I think that they work because of the attraction qualities of the bead more so than the weight.

Q: How do the seasons affect your fishing.
A: I don't fish for spawning fish. The effects of the seasons, for me, are normally different water levels. In the spring there are higher water levels. In the summer, lower water levels and usually somewhat smaller fish.

Q: Does your fly selection change with water type or seasonally?
A: Not as much as you might think. In the spring, I like to fish a red ass for a caddis imitation and in the fall I like to use a Red Ass on the shoals. Often I'll use a Red Ass as a dropper. In the boat, I normally start with a sowbug.

Q: Does your favorite river access change with the seasons?
A: No. I usually put in at Dripping Springs and then move up.

Q: How does the time of day affect your fishing?
A: Usually fishing drops off after lunch.

Q: Do you prefer rising, falling or stable water?
A: Rising water is the best but the benefit doesn't last long. So really slowly falling or stable water is the most dependable.

Q: Are fish signs important to your style of fishing?
A: Absolutely. Always fish to rising fish. They tell you where and what they're eating.

Q: What is your favorite fishing technique? (Swing, strip or dead drift.)
A: Dead drifting is my favorite, although I really like swinging soft hackles.

Q: What has been the biggest change you have seen on the Little Red River?
A: The increase in development and fishing pressure.

Q: What changes do you or don't care for?
A: There is huge pressure on the fishery. It increases every year; which is why I prefer to fish out of a boat. I can still reach less-crowded areas of the river.

Q: Do you ever night fish?
A: No. But I'm going to start. After dark is a big fish time.

Hot Glue Egg

Made by Tom Bly

Hook – Daiichi 1130 Size 14
Body - Orange or Roe colored hot glue. Turn the hook immediately after applying the hot glue to the hook shank to form round shape.

Sowbug

Tied by Tom Bly

Hook – Mustad 3906 Size 14
Thread – 8/0 olive
Weight - .020 lead wire, 12-16 wraps
Shellback – Clear Scud Back
Rib – Tag end of tying thread
Head – Tying thread

Brassie

Originated by Gene Lynch
Tied by Bill Willmert

Hook – Mustad 3906 Size 18
Thread – 8/0 black
Body – Thin gold wire
Rib – Same wire that is used for the body, reverse wrapped
Thorax – Peacock herl
Head – Tying thread

Red Ass

Tied by Tom Bly

Hook – Mustad 3906B
Thread – 8/0 red
Tag – Tying thread
Body – Peacock herl
Hackle – Partridge feather
Head – Tying thread

PT Cruiser

Originated by Tom Bly
Tied by Tom Bly

Hook – Daiichi 1280 Size 18
Bead 5/64 copper bead
Thread – 8/0 red
Tail – Pheasant tail fibers
Rib – Fine copper wire
Body – Pheasant tail fibers, wrapped
Collar – Tying thread

Bob Cotten

"I'm sometimes disappointed when weird and gaudy colored flies catch fish. I want my flies to look natural."

Fly Fishing on the Red

Bob Cotten has fly fished the Little Red River for more than 35 years. Bob fished the Little Red before many of the fly fishermen on the river today were born. Bob may have caught more big browns on the river than any one. Bob specializes in fishing for big brown trout.

Bob fished the river when there was little fishing pressure and has witnessed the river's changes that, unfortunately, are associated with increased pressure and development.

Bob fishes for brown trout during the spawn. This is a time for big fish. One could say that anyone that fishes from October through November on the Little Red is fishing for spawning fish.

One thing that distinguishes Bob from a lot of other people who fish the river during this time is his respect for the resource. Bob handles his fish with care and treats them with respect. He feels strongly that the fisherman must have a moral commitment to the animal he pursues.

Interview:

Q: How long have you fished the Red River?
A: I started fly fishing the Little Red in 1975.

Q: How long have you trout fished?
A: I fly fished the White River a few times on vacation before I started fishing the Little Red seriously.

Q: What did you or do you do in your non fishing life?
A: I worked for 23 years for a trucking company. The last 10 years I ran an air freight company. I retired when I was 58. I'm 78 now.

Q: Have you fly fished for other fish than trout?
A: I started fly fishing for brim and bass at Bear Creek Lake at Crowley's Ridge. I have fished for salmon and trout in Alaska and for a while made annual trips there.

Q: How has this influenced your trout fishing?
A: Brim and bass fishing hasn't seriously influenced my trout fishing. Fishing in Alaska gave me immediate experience in fighting big fish, but really hasn't changed how I like to fish for trout.

Q: What do you look for in selecting a piece of water to fish?
A: I like to fish moving water; especially tailouts. I also think that it is important to look over the water before fishing it. Don't start fishing right away. Look for seams and edges.

Q: Who has influenced your fishing and how?
A: When I started fly fishing the Little Red, there were very few fly fishermen to learn from. When I started, I used a vise grips for a vise. I got most of my information in the beginning from a book called <u>Fly Fishing and Fly Tying</u> by Roy Ovington. But, the one person who influenced my fishing the most was Duane Hada. He owned the first fly shop in Heber Springs. (Note: Duane Hada is also featured in this publication.)

Q: Do you primarily wade or boat fish?
A: I wade 99% of the time. Actually, I hate to boat fish.

Q: Do you use a wading staff?
A: No.

Q: What times of day do you primarily fish?
A: I like to start at first light; when you can barely see.

Q: Do you fish high water?
A: I prefer not to fish high water. But...when I do I use an 11-foot leader, flies with a lot of flash and I use a lot of weight.

Q: What are your favorite flies?
A: I like several flies: a Wooly Bugger, San Juan Worm, and a sowbug tied with squirrel fur. One of my favorite flies is a Size 14 Hare's Ear. I really like to dry fly fish. I tie a CDC Caddis that works pretty well. I also make a "fly" by melting a bead on a small hook. I use that "fly" a lot in the fall.

Q: How do you fish them?
A: I almost always dead drift. I only strip streamers.

Q: Does fly color matter?
A: It does to me. I'm sometimes disappointed when weird and gaudy colored flies catch fish. I want my flies to look natural.

Q: Do you use any special leaders or rigs for your favorite flies?
A: Usually not. But every now and then I'll fish a Wooly Bugger with an indicator. This can be a really effective technique, dead drifting through a run, when swinging a fly doesn't work.

Q: Does your leader change with different flies?
A: No, not really. I generally use a 9-foot leader for a majority of my fishing. Once in a while I'll use a 7X tippet when I'm fishing at the dam.

Q: Do you use fluorocarbon?
A: I sometimes use fluorocarbon tippets on bright days when fishing gets tough.

Q: Do you use strike indicators? What kind?
A: I use strike indicators all the time. My favorites are the little balls with the tooth picks.

Q: What size fly do you fish most often?
A: I probably use a Size 14 Hare's Ear the most, but, I also fish a Size 18 Hare's Ear quite a bit.

Q: What kind of knots do you use?
A: I use a cinch knot to tie the fly to the tippet and a blood knot to connect the tippet to the leader.

Q: What is your favorite piece of equipment?
A: My favorite piece of equipment is my Sage 9-foot, 4-weight DS 2 rod.

Q: What tips or advice would you give a first time fisherman on the Red River?
A: Learn to read the water. Learn how to fish a dead drift. (Without drag.)

Q: What's your favorite rod, reel and line combination?
A: My 9-foot, 4-weight Sage DS 2 with 4-weight forward floating line. I don't have any brand preference with respect to the reel.

Q: Do you tie your own flies?
A: I tie most of the flies that I use.

Q: Do you design your own flies?
A: I tie a CDC Caddis, an egg pattern with a melted bead body and a realistic sowbug. I use a bead head with the egg pattern because it is the most effective way to weight it.

Q: What about bead heads?
A: For the most part, I really don't like bead heads. I think that they are gimmicks.

Q: How do the seasons affect your fishing.
A: July and August are the doldrums. I like to fish for spawning rainbows in September. The browns start in the middle of November and run all the way to January.

Q: Does your fly selection change with water type or seasonally?
A: I like to fish eggs in the fall. But, I'll use a Size 14 Hare's Ear 90-percent of the time. I caught my biggest Red River fish, a 36" Brown, on a Size 14 Hare's Ear.

Q: Does your favorite river access change with the seasons?
A: I like to fish Cow Shoals in the fall.

Q: How does the time of day affect your fishing?
A: I prefer mornings. Early mornings.

Q: Do you prefer rising, falling or stable water?
A: I think that rising water is the best fishing by far. I really don't like to fish falling water.

Q: Are fish signs important to your style of fishing?
A: Absolutely. Every fisherman should know that rising fish are important in locating fishing spots.

Q: What is your favorite fishing technique? (Swing, strip or dead drift.)
A: Dead drifting.

Q: What has been the biggest change you have seen on the Little Red River?
A: No doubt, the biggest change has been the increase in fishing pressure.

Q: What changes do you or don't care for?
A: THE PRESSURE!

Q: Do you ever night fish?
A: No, I really don't enjoy it. I like to see the hit.

Bob Cotton Sowbug

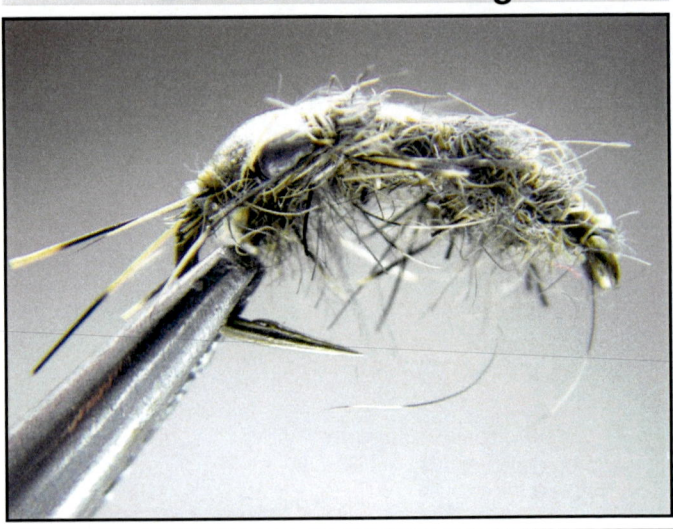

Originated by Bob Cotten
Tied by Bob Cotten

Hook – Mustad 3906 or 3906B Sizes 14 to 18
Weight – 8-10 wraps of .020 lead wire
Thread – 8/0 grey or olive
Rib – Tag end of the tying thread
Body – Dubbed squirrel hair
Shellback – Clear plastic cut from a plastic bag or Scudback
Head – Tying thread.

CDC Caddis

Originated by Bob Cotten
Tied by Bob Cotten

Hook – Mustad 94840 Sizes 14 to 18
Thread – 8/0 olive
Body – Olive or brown Antron
Wing – One or two natural or grey CDC feathers tied in over the hook shank and trimmed to size.
Head – Tying thread

Egg Fly Pattern

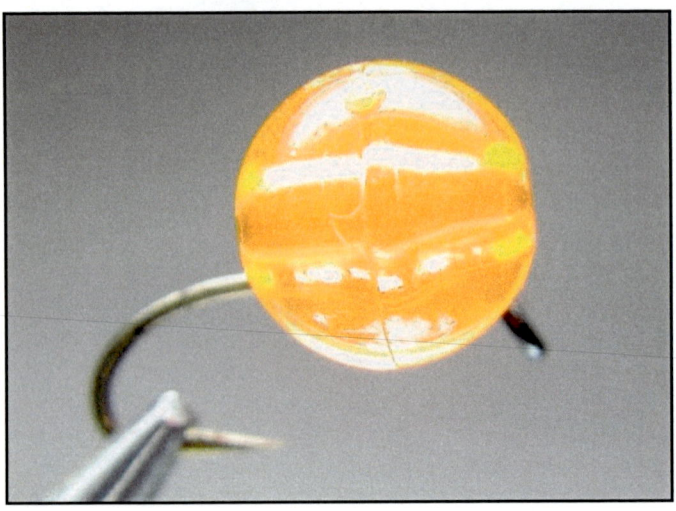

Originated by Bob Cotten
Made by Bob Cotten

Hook – Bob uses a variety of hooks. Any wet fly or nymph hook can be used. Typically recommended is a glow bug or a caddis style hook. Suitable hooks would include the following hooks in the Mustad line: 9174, 9479, R48, 80200BR, and 81001BR. Sizes 14 to 18.

    Bob orders his beads from a fly shop in Alaska. He says that the right color bead is critical. With the popularity of "pegged bead" fishing styles, many fly shops carry beads of various sizes in "fishy colors."
    To make the fly, Bob clamps a hook in his vise, heats the hook shank for two seconds, and presses the bead onto the hook.

Chuck Farneth

Any fishing experience will help you develop your skills. It is especially important learning how to handle and land big fish on light tackle.

Charles (Chuck) Farneth has fly fished for more than 40 years. Starting at an early age in his hometown of New Kensington, Penn., Chuck spent much of his youth fishing for trout and other species in western and central Pennsylvania.

Through careers as a Tow Boat Captain for 13 years on the Three Rivers in Pittsburgh, a manufacturing operations planner and a 10-year stint with the Campus Crusade for Christ, Chuck continued to fish and learn in streams from Alaska to Connecticut.

Chuck has been a fishing and casting instructor, a fishing guide and organized and managed fly fishing retreats and outings. His fishing prowess has netted him local, regional and national fishing and casting awards. Chuck competed on ESPN in the Great Outdoor Games. In 2000 he finished with a Bronze medal in casting distance and accuracy. In 2001, Chuck finished first in the One Fish Competition and in 2002, took a Bronze medal in the same category. In 2004, Chuck finished first in the OLN Fly Fishing Masters in the Northeast Region team event held at Lake Placid, NY.

Currently, owner (with his wife Sherry) of Driftwood Lodge, a bed and breakfast on the Little Red River, and Founder and Executive Director of Outdoor Legacy, Chuck still finds time to guide and fish on the Little Red, White and North Fork of the White rivers.

Interview:

Q: How long have you fished the Little Red River?
A: Since 1994.

Q: How long have you trout fished?
A: I started trout fishing in Pennsylvania when I was 6 years old.

Q: What do you do in your non-fishing life?
A: Currently I manage and direct Outdoor Legacy, a non-denominational ministry that uses outdoor activities

as a means to focus on family and Biblical principles of manhood. I also run Driftwood lodge with my wife, Sherry, and guide for trout part-time on the Little Red and Norfork Rivers.

Q: Have you fly fished for other fish than trout?
A: In freshwater I have fished for trout, salmon, steelhead, pike, muskies, carp, and both largemouth and smallmouth bass. In saltwater, I have fished for bonefish, permit, tarpon and redfish.

Q: How has this influenced your trout fishing?
A: Any fishing experience will help you develop your skills. This is especially important in learning how to handle and land big fish on light tackle.

Q: What do you look for in selecting a piece of water to fish?
A: I like to fish deeper water with some kind of cover for larger fish, but for an easy catch I'll always fish moving water.

Q: Do you primarily wade or boat fish?
A: I like to wade because I can work more closely with my clients. I have the freedom to teach casting and various fishing techniques.

Q: Do you use a wading staff?
A: No, I really don't need one on the Little Red.

Q: What times of day do you primarily fish?
A: I like the mornings the best: 10 a.m. to 1 p.m. is probably my favorite time.

Q: Do you fish high water?
A: Fishing low water is more interesting because you can use so many more techniques. You can fish dry flies, midges or emergers. Dry flies can be especially effective in low water. You can also use more finesse presentations.

Q: How does this influence your fishing?
A: Deeper and slower water forces you to be more patient, more technical and at times use longer drifts to cover more water. In general, this water requires more finesse.

Q: What are your favorite flies?
A: I like to fish mayfly nymphs, midge pupae, caddis emergers or dry flies the best.

Q: How do you fish them?
A: Normally I'll fish under an indicator unless I'm fishing an emerger, streamer or tight-lining nymphs.

Q: Do you use any special leaders or rigs for your favorite flies?
A: I really like Froghair's 12-foot George Harvey leader.

Q: Do you use strike indicators? What kind?
A: I use Palsa or Froghair indicators. They are easy to see and especially easy to put on and take off.

Q: What size fly do you fish most often?
A: Generally Size 16 or 18.

Q: Does fly color matter?
A: Yes, in low light conditions I favor darker flies, while in brighter conditions, I like to use lighter patterns.

Q: Do you use fluorocarbon?
A: I always use fluorocarbon tippets. I think that Froghair makes the best fluorocarbon material.

Q: Does your leader change with different flies?
A: Yes, I'll use a heavier, shorter leader with streamers. I vary my tippet with different size flies. Larger flies require a heavier tippet, with lighter flies I generally use a lighter and longer tippet.

Q: What kind of knots do you use.

A: To join sections of leader I use a blood knot or a ligature knot. To tie the fly onto the tippet I'll use either a Pitzen (16-20) or a Eugene Bend knot.

Q: What tips or advice would you give a first time fisherman on the Red River?
A: Wade as little as possible. One mistake that beginning fishermen make, is that they often wade through the fish before they even start fishing. Most fishermen would catch more fish if they would learn to improve their casting. Some fishermen can't cast far enough to reach the fish.

Q: What's your favorite rod, reel and line combination?
A: Rod – Chuck Farneth Legacy 9-foot, 4-Weight.
   Reel – Abel Super 5
   Line – Scientific Angler's GPX

Q: Do you tie your own flies?
A: I tie all of the flies that I fish with.

Q: Do you design your own flies?
A: Yes, I have designed many of the patterns that I fish with; from streamers to emergers to midges.

Q: What about bead heads?
A: I use bead heads, but not all the time. I guess that I use bead heads about 50% of the time when I fish moving water or deep pools to get the fly down.

Q: How do the seasons affect your fishing?
A: Spring and fall are the prettiest and most comfortable seasons on the Little Red River. I especially like to fish for brown trout in the fall colors or bright rainbows through the winter.

Q: Does your fly selection change with water type or seasonally?
A: I'll use more midges in the winter and more caddis in the spring. In turbid water I like to use larger flies.

Q: Does your favorite river access change with the seasons?
A: Yes, I'll frequently fish the lower sections of the river when the spring hatches come off. I'll target brown trout in the late summer and early fall before their spawning activity. I do not fish over trout on their redds.

Q: How does the time of day affect your fishing?
A: Fishing usually slows down between 1 and 5 pm.

Q: Do you prefer rising, falling or stable water?
A: I like to fish stable water.

Q: Are fish signs important to your style of fishing?
A: I don't think that they are that important, however fish signs would determine the type of fly that I might use. For example, they would determine whether I would use a dryfly or an emerger.

Q: What is your favorite fishing technique? (Swing, strip or dead drift.)
A: On the Little Red, I'll normally drift flies under an indicator, but dry fly fishing is my hands down favorite.

Q: Do you ever night fish?
A: Yes, with caution. Night fishing is the best time to hunt for big browns.

Q: What has been the biggest change you have seen on the Little Red River?
A: Fishing pressure has increased dramatically on the Red River yearly since I have fished it. I can remember when very few anglers fished Cow Shoals in the fall. Now, on weekends, a quality fishing experience is unusual.

Q: What is your favorite piece of equipment?
A: My reading glasses or magnifiers.

CF Hare's Ear

Originated by Chuck Farneth
Tied by Chuck Farneth

Hook – MFC (Montana Fly Company) 7026 (Similar to Mustad 9671) Size 14 to 20
Head – 5/64 Tungsten bead (gold or black)
Thread – 8/0 Black
Tail – Rabbit guard hairs
Rib – Hollow shimmer (Silky)
Body – Natural hare's ear
Thorax – Natural hare's ear
Head – Tying thread

CF Sowbug

Originated by Chuck Farneth
Tied by Chuck Farneth

Hook – Daiichi 1130 Size 16 to 18
Thread – 8/0 Tan
Tail – Grey goose biot
Rib – Grey monofilament
Shell back split – Peacock quill
Shellback – Tan scudback
Head – Tying thread

Grey Fox Variant

Originated by Art Flick
Tied by Chuck Farneth

Hook – Tiemco 5212 Size 12
Thread – 8/0 Tan
Tail – Brown and grizzly rooster hackle
Body – Brown rooster hackle quill
Hackle – Brown and grizzly rooster hackle
Head – Tying thread

CF Blue Wing Emerger

Originated by Chuck Farneth
Tied by Chuck Farneth

Hook – Tiemco 100BL Size 18 to 22
Thread – 8/0 olive
Tail – Blue dun "stiff" hen hackle
Body – Stripped peacock herl
Hackle – Blue dun "stiff" hen hackle
Head – Tying thread

CF Diving Caddis

Originated by Chuck Farneth
Tied by Chuck Farneth

Hook – Tiemco 100 BL Size 14
Head – Tungsten Bead
Body – Black Thread
Thorax – Peacock
Wing Slips – Mallard wing tips
Wing – Wood duck barbs

Duane Hada

Don't overlook slow moving water. Fish moss beds and holes.

Fly Fishing on the Red

Duane Hada has been associated with big brown trout and fly fishing on the Little Red River since the 1980's. Duane grew up in rural Arkansas, close to Crooked Creek. In those days, he says, family fun was fishing.

When Duane was 14 years old his family moved to Hasty, Ark. There Duane polished his smallmouth bass fishing skills. Duane attended the University of Central Arkansas in Conway in 1981. While a student, he fished the Little Red in Heber regularly. He graduated in 1985 with a BSE in Art. Duane recalls Heber Springs as a sleepy little town in those days.

After graduation, Duane took his first teaching job in Mena, Ark. There he also taught a fly fishing course at Rich Mountain Community College. A student of Duane's opened up an outdoor store, The Woodsman. Duane was soon guiding for the new store.

In 1988, Duane opened up a satellite Woodsman store in Heber Springs. Duane guided and managed the store from 1988 until 1990. In 1990, water ran over the top of the dam and severe flooding and high water were too much for the business.

Duane moved to Fort Smith and again worked for the original Woodsman, guiding on the Little Red, as well as organizing all travel and destination trips for the store. In 1998, Duane moved to Yellville, where Duane's wife, Marlene, taught school. Duane wanted to concentrate on art, but still worked as a guide.

Duane has since opened The River Town Gallery in Cotter, Ark., teaches art at ASU, Mountain Home and continues to apply his skills to painting and fishing.

Interview:

Q: How long have you fished the Little Red River?
A: I've fished the Little Red for 30 years.

Q: How long have you trout fished?
A: I have fly fished for trout for 40 years.

Q: What do you do in your non-fishing life?
A: I've worked as a guide, a teacher and an artist.

Q: Have you fly fished for other fish than trout?
A: I'm still working on my life list. So far, I've caught 118 different species, including some rare cutthroats and several saltwater species. I particularly enjoy fishing for native fish in natural areas. My favorite may be a smallmouth bass. I think the smallmouth really symbolizes the area where I've spent most of my life. The smallmouth is beautiful, hard fighting, and has earned a niche in some pretty rugged country.

Q: How has this influenced your trout fishing?
A: I use quite a few bass techniques for trout. Large flies at night for example. I'll often use large pencil poppers at night for big browns in August.

Q: What do you look for in selecting water to fish?
A: I look for water that has the potential to hold a big fish. I like dark moss beds or holes with wood cover. I fish water that looks "bassy" for trout.

Q: Who has influenced your fishing and how?
A: Dave Whitlock and I are good friends. We have known each other for years. Good friends can't fish together without sharing ideas. Another influence was Kevin Short. Kevin guides for me and used to fish on a bass circuit. He was very successful finding and catching big fish.

Q: Do you primarily wade or boat fish?
A: I prefer to fish out of a canoe. I like to sight fish while poling a canoe.

Q: Do you use a wading staff?
A: No.

Q: What times of day do you primarily fish?
A: Mornings. I like to have enough light to see well. I think that this is the best light for sight fishing.

Q: Do you fish high water?
A: Not usually. I'll occasionally fish high water with clients. Then, I'll concentrate on back pockets in the bank. An example of this water would be next to Canoe Creek on the Little Red. Fish will move up into the shallow water and be tailing, eating sowbugs.

Q: What are your favorite flies?
A: My first choice would be a sowbug, followed by a Pheasant Tail. Gray and black midges work well at the dam. For a streamer, I'd pick a Zonker. A local dentist used to tie a nymph called an El Lobo nymph that used to work pretty well. Dan Baily sold a grey Woolly Worm with gray dental dam pulled over the back. It looked like a sowbug, only three times bigger. Frank Brown and Abe Vogel tied some of the first natural sowbugs. They had a tail made out of goose biots, a body made of dubbing from a carpet, that held its color in the water, its body was flattened, and had a back of clear plastic.

Q: How do you fish them?
A: My preferred method is sight casting to the fish. I think that indicator fishing may be the most effective technique.

Q: Does fly color matter?
A: Yes. For big fish I think you should match the color of the natural foods. Stockers will hit the weird colors readily.

Q: Do you use any special leaders or rigs for your favorite flies?
A: I started using double-stick tape for an indicator on a 12- to 14-foot leader and the lightest tippet possible. I would use 5X the most.

Q: Does your leader change with different flies?
A: For streamers I use a 9-foot, 3X tippet. For nymphs I like a right-angle leader that I saw on the San Juan, with an indicator made of Antron yarn.

Q: Do you use fluorocarbon?
A: No, I don't like its stiffness and the fact that it does not stretch.

Q: Do you use strike indicators? What kind?
A: Rolled double stick tape.

Q: What size fly do you fish most often?
A: Sowbugs - Size 12 to 14
   Zonkers - Size 6

Q: What kind of knots do you use?
A: Fly to tippet – Improved cinch
   Tippet to leader – Double surgeons knot
   Leader to fly line – Nail-less nail knot

Q: What is your favorite piece of equipment?
A: A 9-foot Sage Light Line, 5-weight rod.

Q: What tips or advice would you give a first time fisherman on the Red River?
A: Do not overlook slow moving water. Fish moss beds and holes.

Q: What's your favorite rod, reel and line combination?
A: The Sage 5-weight Light Line rod, with a Ross Evolution reel and a 5-weight floating line.

Q: Do you tie your own flies?
A: Yes.

Q: Do you design your own flies?
A: Yes. Hada's Creek Crawler is an Umpqua pattern.

Q: What about bead heads?
A: I use them on Woolly Buggers and caddis nymphs. I do not use them on sowbugs.

Q: How do the seasons affect your fishing.
A: In March and April I start fishing further downstream. I like to fish those areas for caddis and sulpher hatches.

Q: Does your fly selection change with water type or seasonally?
A: I mimic the most prolific food source of the season. An example would be during the pre-spawn period I'll use streamers, while in winter I like to use a lot of midges.

Q: Does your favorite river access change with the seasons?
A: In late spring I like to fish down river more. There are more hatches there, and a lot less pressure.

Q: How does the time of day affect your fishing?
A: From the aspect of light, high bright light is hard on the big browns. It makes fishing tougher.

Q: Do you prefer rising, falling or stable water?
A: My favorite is stable water. My least favorite is falling water.

Q: Are fish signs important to your style of fishing?
A: You need the rise forms to help you select a fly.

Q: What is your favorite fishing technique? (Swing, strip or dead drift.)
A: Dead drifting to sighted fish.

Q: What has been the biggest change you have seen on the Little Red River?
A: Over development.

Q: What changes do you or don't care for?
A: Certainly over harvest.

Q: Do you ever night fish?
A: Yes. That is the best time to fish for big fish.

Pheasant Tail

*Originated by Frank Sawer – Al Troth Version
Tied by Bill Willmert*

Hook – Mustad R70 Size 18
Thread 8/0 black
Tail – 3-4 Pheasant tail fibers
Rib – Copper wire
Body – Palmered pheasant tail fibers
Wing Case – Pheasant tail fibers left over from wrapping the body
Thorax – Peacock herl
Head – Tying thread

Zonker

Originated by Dan Byford
Tied by Bill Willmert

Hook – Mustad 9674 Size 8
Thread – 8/0 olive
Body – Silver mylar tubing
Wing – Chartreuse rabbit strip
Collar – Olive mallard flank
Head – Tying thread

Jeff Hawthorne

Check with a local fly shop for local water conditions, where to fish and what patterns are working.

Jeff Hawthorne runs the Ozark Angler in Heber Springs. He also guides more than 150 days a year on the Little Red River, ties thousands of dozens of several varieties of flies and nets over 6,000 fish every year. Jeff may know the river better than anyone else who fishes here.

His face is constantly sun-burned, but always equipped with a happy, friendly, glad-to-see-ya smile. Any visitor to his shop gets a friendly greeting and, as often as not, a quick fishing tip or report. Even a short visit leaves the visitor feeling just a little bit better.

Many of the experienced fishermen on the river say that Jeff is the first guide that they would hire or recommend because Jeff's clients have fun.

Jeff says that catching fish is never enough. Jeff wants to teach his clients something about fishing to take home with them. More importantly, Jeff works as hard as any guide on the river to ensure that his clients have a good time.

Good stories, good cigars, and good food, depending on the client, can make the difference between a good trip and a great trip. Anyone who fishes with Jeff knows that, too.

Interview:

Q. How long have you trout fished on the Little Red River?
A. 14 years.

Q. What did you do in your non-fishing life?
A. I managed a golf course in Florida for 15 years.

Q. Have you fly fished for fish other than trout?
A. Yes, I've fly fished for bonefish, smallmouth bass and billfish offshore.

Q. How has this influenced your trout fishing?
A. I learned to fish many different patterns, especially streamers.

Q. What do you look for in selecting a piece of water to fish?
A. I like to fish moving water. There are more bugs in moving water and the fish are usually more active. You can't get a good drift without a current.

Q. Who has influenced your fly fishing?
A. Bill Combs and Tom Hawthorne. I learned the Little Red from Bill. Bill got me started tying flies, my brother Tom really gave me a start fly fishing for trout. (Note: Tom Hawthorne is also featured in this publication.)

Q. Do you primarily wade or boat fish?
A. I like to wade, but most of my guiding is from a boat.

Q. Do you use a wading staff?
A. No.

Q. What time of day do you primarily fish?
A. I fish all day when I'm guiding. My favorite time to fish is in the last light of the day, the last three to four hours before dark.

Q. Do you fish high water?
A. I don't guide in extremely high water. I really don't enjoy fishing in high water. If I fish in high water I use a sink tip and large streamers.

Q. What are your favorite flies?
A. My three favorite flies are sowbugs, midges and a Red Ass.

Q. How do you fish them?
A. Normally, I like to fish them on a dead drift. Dead drifting nymphs and sowbugs is a good technique to introduce people to fly fishing.

Q. Do you use any special leaders or rigs for your favorite flies?
A. I like to use floating leaders for a longer drift. Float-

ing leaders help avoid micro drag, they are easier to mend, and they'll float ahead of the leader.

Q. Do you use strike indicators?
A. Yes, I like Palsa the best, in orange.

Q. Does fly color matter?
A. Absolutely. I like to use flashy, darker flies in colored water. In clear water I use smaller flies.

Q. Do you use fluorocarbon?
A. I use regular mono-filament for leaders. Fluorocarbon just sinks too fast. I do use fluorocarbon for almost all of my tippets.

Q. Does your leader change with different flies?
A. I only change my leader for fishing streamers. Then I fish 6- to 8-pound test regular monofilament leaders.

Q. What kind of knots do you use?
A. For tippets I'll use a double surgeons knot. For nymphs I like a double surgeons loop, and for dry flies, a cinch knot seems to work the best for me.

Q. What tips or advice would you give a first time fisherman to the Little Red River?
A. Check with a local fly shop for local water conditions, where to fish and what patterns are working. Make sure that you are fishing deep enough; (bounce the bottom). When fishing public access points, swing your flies. You can use weighted sowbugs for weight.

Q. What's your favorite rod and reel combination?
A. Rod – Five weight Winston IIBX
    Reel – Ross Gunnison
    Line - Rio Weight Forward floating line.

Q. What is your favorite piece of equipment?
A. First, I'd have to say, without question, my boat. I can get away from public access points and of course I

cover much more water with a boat. Secondly, I'd say my Ketchum Release tool. I think that this tool really minimizes handling fish that are going to be released. The survivability of the fish is significantly improved.

Q. Do you tie your own flies?
A. Yes, every single one. I tie over 1,200 dozen flies per year.

Q. Do you design your own flies?
A. Yes, I designed the "Candy Cane" (a soft hackle on a 2X nymph hook). The" Extra Crispy" is also one of my flies. I also tie and fish the "Purple Haze" which was originated by Tom Gazaway.

Q. What about bead heads?
A. I like bead heads a lot. Bead heads are good attractors and add weight to any pattern. Gold and silver tend to be my favorites. Copper works really well on the White River.

Q. How do the seasons affect your fishing?
A. I love fishing in the winter. There are fewer people; you can usually have the river all to yourself. Spring and fall are great times to fish the Little Red. They are the prettiest time on the river. April, May and June are the trickiest times to fish the river because of inconsistent generation patterns.

Q. Does your fly selection change with water type or the seasons?
A. I like to fish nymphs during the winter. In the spring I love fishing the caddis hatches. My favorite spring flies are an Elk Hair Caddis, a Red Ass and a dry with a dropper.

Q. Does your favorite river access change with the seasons?
A. I like to fish the lower sections of the river, (below Swinging Bridge) once the hatches start.

Q. How does the time of day affect your fishing?
A. There seems to be a dead zone between 11 a.m. to 1 p.m. I think that mornings are slower than afternoons.

Q. Do you prefer rising, falling or stable water?
A. Generally I like falling water the best. When the water is rising you usually end up with too much water.

Q. Are fish signs important to your style of fishing?
A. Fish signs are extremely important. You need to find active fish and fish signs will generally show you how the fish are feeding. Then match your presentation accordingly.

Q. What is your favorite fishing technique? (Swing, strip or dead drift)
A. Most of the time I prefer to present my flies on a dead drift.

Q. What has been the biggest change you have seen on the Little Red River?
A. Over time, siltation has been the biggest change with the worst effect. This has really damaged fishing by covering up rocks and smothering insects. This seems to be an effect of the continued development on the river.

Q. Do you ever night fish?
A. Yes, but I really don't care for it much.

Candy Cane

Originated by Jeff Hawthorne
Tied by Jeff Hawthorne

Hook – Mustad 3906B Size 16 to 14
Thread – 8/0 red
Rib – Red Krystal Flash
Body – Silver Krystal Flash
Hackle – Partridge
Head – Tying thread

Purple Haze

Originated by Tom Gazaway
Tied by Jeff Hawthorne

Hook – Daiichi 1130 Size 14
Thread – 8/0 olive
Bead – 7/64" Gold bead
Rib - Tying thread tag end
Shellback – Clear Scud Back
Body – UV tan ice dubbing

Extra Crispy

Originated by Jeff Hawthorne
Tied by Jeff Hawthorne

Hook – Daiichi – 1130 Size 14
Bead 7/64" Gold bead
Thread – 8/0 olive
Body – Golden brown Ice dubbing

Tom Hawthorne

Be patient. Patience is your best friend. Keep your fly in the water. Near the dam you can fish a cast for 5 minutes.

Tom Hawthorne learned to fly fish for trout in 1979 and 1980 while working in Utah as a helicopter mechanic.

Soon after, he began guiding, fishing Yellowstone Park and Jackson Hole, Wyoming, as well as various rivers in Utah and Idaho. Tom moved to Little Rock in 1984.

In 1985, he fished Alaska and that same year, started selling his flies. Tom continued to pick up orders and was soon selling brim flies in Arkansas. The Ozark Angler shop in Heber Springs started as part of Tom's commercial fly-tying business. Tom owned and directed the Ozark Angler for the more than 20 years.

He sold the shop in late 2008 but is still active as a consultant and guide. Tom Hawthorne is thoughtful and careful in his responses and clearly shows the deep feeling and care he has for the Little Red River fishery. For example, he won't allow guides working for him to target and fish for spawning brown trout.

Interview:

Q: How long have you fished the Red River?
A: I have fished the Little Red River since 1984.

Q: How long have you trout fished?
A: I started fly fishing for trout in 1979. I guess that's 30 years.

Q: What did you do in your non-fishing life?
A: I was a helicopter mechanic.

Q: Have you fly fished for other fish than trout?
A: Sure. I've fly fished for salmon, bonefish and marlin.

Q: How has this influenced your trout fishing?
A: I'm not really sure that saltwater fly fishing has influenced my trout fishing in any way except that it has improved my skill set. It certainly has improved my casting.

Q: What do you look for in selecting a piece of water to fish?
A: When I'm nymphing, I prefer heavy water; boulders with plenty of pocket water. When I dry fly fish, I like to fish really long drifts from a boat.

Q: Who has influenced your fishing and how?
A: My mentor was Ted Angle. I'm also quite a fan of Charles Brooks. I fished with Charles Brooks on the Yellowstone River.

Q: Do you primarily wade or boat fish?
A: I get hot and cold on both. I like to wade alone but really I think that I prefer boat fishing.

Q: Do you use a wading staff?
A: Never. At least, not yet.

Q: What times of day do you primarily fish?
A: I'm really a dry fly person, so I'd say from 9-10 a.m. until 1-2 p.m. are my favorite times.

Q: Do you fish high water?
A: Some. I really don't mind fishing high water. Anything over dead, flat, low water! When I fish high water I use big flies, Size 2's and Double Bunnies.

Q: What are your favorite flies?
A: For a dry fly I like the Parachute Adams. My favorite wet fly is the Red Ass. The Red Ass is an English pattern. The Red Ass Kelso is its full name. I learned about the fly in Dillion, Montana. I may have introduced the pattern here. I brought it back with me 1985.

Q: How do you fish them?
A: Well, as I said, I like drys the best.

Q: Does fly color matter?
A: At least from the surface to 3 feet under. But I think that shape is more important than either size or color.

Q: Do you use any special leaders or rigs for your favorite flies?
A: I do. I tie my own leaders. I like to use George Harvey's Slack line leader, especially for dry flies or midges.

Q: Does your leader change with different flies?
A: Yes, I fish a heavier leader than most. Generally 3X-4X, instead of 5X-6X. I want some line for a big fish.

Q: Do you use fluorocarbon?
A: Yes. I use it in very shallow or clear water. I don't use it in off color water though. I don't like how it isn't good for the environment. It doesn't biodegrade. I don't throw away scrap broken sections or leaders. I try to be very careful about that.

Q: Do you use strike indicators? What kind?
A: Yes. When I'm with customers I use the pinch on type. When I fish by myself, I like to use yarn indicators.

Q: What size fly do you fish most often?
A: Size 14.

Q: What kind of knots do you use?
A: For dry flies I use a figure-8 knot. For nymphs I use a double surgeons knot. (Tom popularized this knot here. To get a small loop stick the eye of the hook back through the loop and pull the tag ends until the loop is the size that you want).

Q: What is your favorite piece of equipment?
A: I just love reels. The old Loops with no drag and the classic CFO's are some of my favorites. I landed a 43-pound salmon on a 6-weight rod with a #2 Loop reel. The new Sage reels are wonderfully engineered.

Q: What tips or advice would you give a first-time fisherman on the Red River?
A: Be patient. Patience is your best friend. Keep your

fly in the water. Near the dam you can fish a cast for five minutes.

Q: What's your favorite rod, reel and line combination?
A: I think that a 9-foot, 4-weight rod with a floating line would be my pick for the Little Red River. I have favorites in all brands so I can't really pick one. I do love bamboo rods, though. One of my favorite bamboo rods would be an Orvis 99, built on a Wes Jorden taper. Another rod, is a 7-foot, 4-weight copy of a 2012 Dickerson that Tony Austin built for me.

Q: Do you tie your own flies?
A: Yes.

Q: Do you design your own flies?
A: No, I'm not a great fly designer. I usually tie for the store or for a special trip.

Q: What about bead heads?
A: I think that they are wonderful. They put the weight in just the right spot.

Q: How do the seasons affect your fishing?
A: Steady flows are more important than the season. My least favorite time is in the fall during the brown trout spawn. I don't think that we should be fishing over spawning browns.

Q: Does your fly selection change with water type or seasonally?
A: Definitely. In April I like to fish the caddis hatches. In summer, I don't think that it matters all that much because there are so many hatchery fish. In the winter I fish midges mostly.

Q: Does your favorite river access change with the seasons?
A: Yes, usually I like to fish from Lobo downstream. Later, in the fall I'll usually pick Ramsey or Dripping Springs because the flows are more stable.

Q: How does the time of day affect your fishing?
A: High bright sunlight is tough for big fish. I like to fish at dawn or dusk for big fish.

Q: Do you prefer rising, falling or stable water?
A: Really, if there is no generation, all the water is falling. Falling or stable water is easier to fish, especially for dry flies.

Q: Are fish signs important to your style of fishing?
A: I tell my students to let the fish tell you how and what they are feeding on. Then, pick your fly accordingly. You have to watch and pay attention.

Q: What is your favorite fishing technique? (Swing, strip or dead drift.)
A: I like to fish dry flies to rising fish the best. Some of the most exciting fishing I've done was fishing a mouse pattern on the top for big rainbows in Alaska.

Q: What has been the biggest change you have seen on the Little Red River?
A: Increased development has caused a huge increase in the siltation of the river bottom. There is silt everywhere now. Over time there has been a steady increase in fishing pressure on the river.

Q: What changes do you or don't you care for?
A: With the increase of fishing pressure, a lot more people are fishing the brown trout spawn. I think the spawn should be protected. Large fish need protection. Fishing over spawning fish is primarily responsible for the decline in quality brown trout fishing. There has been a huge decline in the size of our brown trout.

Q. Do you ever night fish?
A. I hate it.

Parachute Adams

Tied by Bill Willmert

Hook – Tiemco 100 Size 16
Thread - 8/0 grey
Tail – Grizzley hackle fibers
Wing – White calf tail
Body – Muskrat fur
Hackle – Brown and grizzly hackle wound together
Head – Tying thread

Double Bunny

Originated by Scott Sanchez
Tied by Bill Willmert

Hook – Mustad 79580 Size 4
Thread – 6/0 white
Weight - .020 lead wire, 10-12 wraps, wrapped on the front half of the hook
Body – Chartreuse rabbit strip for the back and a white rabbit strip for the belly.
Note – The rabbit strips are glued to the hook and each other with contact cement.
Flash – Three to five strips of pearl Flashabou
Eyes – 4 mm Safety Eyes or Real Eyes

Donnie Hyslip

Don't wade through fish that you want to cast to. Many people wade through areas that they ought drift their flies through.

Donnie Hyslip was born in east Arkansas in 1947. He started fly fishing for bream and bass while he worked for the National Guard in Marianna, Ark. When Donnie moved to Conway in 1987, he started fly fishing the Little Red River. He retired from the National Guard in 1995 and moved to Heber Springs with his wife, Ruth.

He took up part time work for the Ozark Angler in 1996, and in 1998, began taking clients as a guide. Donnie continued to guide for Ozark Angler until 2002 and also guided independently from 2002 until 2005.

Donnie is currently a Certified Casting Instructor with the FFF. He worked for the Little Red Fly Shop from 2006 to 2010 teaching casting and fly tying.

Interview:

Q: How long have you fished the Little Red River?
A: I've fished the Little Red for 24 years.

Q: How long have you trout fished?
A: 24 Years.

Q: What did you do in your non-fishing life?
A: I worked as a technician for the National Guard.

Q: Have you fly fished for other fish than trout?
A: I have fly fished for bream, catfish, crappie, white bass, walleye, and smallmouth.

Q: How has this influenced your trout fishing?
A: While fishing for catfish, I learned the importance of fishing steamers slowly. I think that most people fish streamers like Woolly Buggers too fast for trout.

Q: What do you look for in selecting water to fish?
A: I look for structure, rocks, cuts in the bank, and drop offs.

Q: Who has influenced your fishing and how?

A: I watch other people fishing. I learn a lot that way. As an author, Mel Krieger has had a big influence on my casting.

Q: Do you primarily wade or boat fish?
A: I previously, primarily boat fished. I wade more and more now.

Q: Do you use a wading staff?
A: Not yet. I think they are noisy.

Q: What times of day do you primarily fish?
A: Anytime. I really don't have a favorite time.

Q: Do you fish high water?
A: Obviously, only in a boat. In high water, fish bigger and deeper. I like to use a San Juan Worm dropper off of a micro jig.

Q: What are your favorite flies?
A: Sowbugs and San Juan Worms are some of my favorite flies. My favorite colors for the San Juan Worms are red, fluorescent cerise and brown.

Q: How do you fish them?
A: Dead drifting under an indicator.

Q: Does fly color matter?
A: To some extent. Here's a short list of colors that I prefer for sowbugs: light tan Antron, Callibaetis super fine dubbing, light hare's ear combined with Antron, and brown. I also use a lot of Sow Scud dubbing.

Q: Do you use any special leaders or rigs for your favorite flies?
A: I generally use a 9-foot, 5X leader. I'll cut a foot off the end and tie on 3- to 4-feet of 5X fluorocarbon tippet. For streamers I like to use 6- to 8-feet of 3X tippet. I'll use a perfection loop to connect the leader to the fly line.

Q: Does your leader change with different flies?
A: No.

Q: Do you use fluorocarbon?
A: I always use fluorocarbon for tippets.

Q: Do you use strike indicators? What kind?
A: Yes. When I'm fishing 3-feet deep or less, I use a Palsa stick-on indicator. When I fish deeper than 3 feet, I tie on a piece of Loon Strike II yarn.

Q: What size fly do you fish most often?
A: Size 14

Q: What kind of knots do you use.
A: Tippet to Leader – double surgeons knot
    Tippet to fly – surgeons loop knot

Q: What is your favorite piece of equipment?
A: A Thomas and Thomas 8.5-foot, 4-weight rod.

Q: What tips or advice would you give a first time fisherman on the Red River?
A: Do less wading and less casting and spend more time looking. Don't wade through fish that you want to cast to. So many people wade through areas that they ought drift their flies through.

Q: What's your favorite rod, reel and line combination?
A: Thomas and Thomas 8.5-foot, 4-weight rod, a Bauer M2 reel and a 4-weight floating WF Rio line.

Q: Do you tie your own flies?
A: Yes.

Q: Do you design your own flies?
A: Some. I have a pattern under consideration for inclusion in Rainy's Catalog. It's called a LRFS Soft Hackle. LRFS stands for Little Red Fly Shop. For my personal fishing, I like to use anatomically correct flies.

(Flies that resemble the natural as opposed to general attractors.)

Q: What about bead heads?
A: I like bead heads.

Q: How do the seasons affect your fishing.
A: In the summer I like to fish the deeper pools. In the winter, if river traffic is low, I usually like to fish the shallows.

Q: Does your fly selection change with water type or seasonally?
A: When I fish deeper water, I use darker flies. In shallow water, I like lighter flies.

Q: Does your favorite river access change with the seasons?
A: I like to fish the dam in the winter. The deeper pools there hold big fish. In the summer, I like some of the deeper pools below Winkley.

Q: How does the time of day affect your fishing?
A; I prefer to face the sun while fishing. I want to avoid making shadows.

Q: Do you prefer rising, falling or stable water?
A: Stable water is best for wading. When boat fishing I like water on a slow rise. It can be the very best water, although it doesn't usually last long.

Q: Are fish signs important to your style of fishing?
A: I always stop and fish to rising fish.

Q: What is your favorite fishing technique? (Swing, strip or dead drift.)
A: Dead drifting.

Q: What has been the biggest change you have seen on the Little Red River?

A: Pools are silting in and the river is getting wider.

Q: What changes do you or don't care for?
A: The uncontrolled development is causing a lot of problems on the river.

Q: Do you ever night fish?
A: No.

San Juan Worm

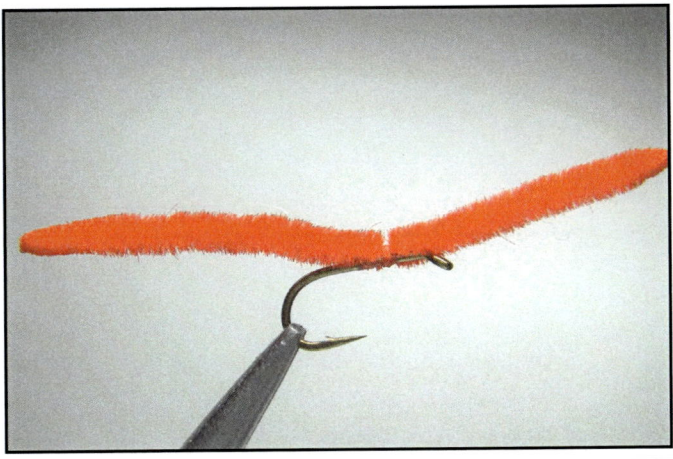

Tied by Bill Willmert

Hook – R70 Size 16
Thread- 8/0 red
Body – Pink vernile

Micro Jig

Tied by Bill Willmert

Hook – 128th ounce jig hook
Thread – 8/0 red
Flash – Two strands of silver Krystal Flash
Body – White marabou tied on top of the hook shank
Collar – Red tying thread

Jack Kirby

The first thing that I look for is privacy. That's getting tougher all the time.

Jack Kirby fishes the Little red River like no one else. First of all, Jack is on the water between 150 to 250 days every year. One of his favorite quips is that, "In the beginning I used to follow the herons, now they follow me."

Over the years, Jack developed some innovative techniques for fishing his favorite stretches of river. He is frequently seen in his boat, the Dirt Dauber. But he also wades the river in a float tube. That's right: he's wading ... not wearing the fins generally used to steer a float tube. If he steps into a hole or loses his footing, he'll be sitting, floating in the tube. Wearing a float tube without fins is unconventional. Then again walking is infinitely easier wearing boots instead of fins.

But walking a tube isn't the most unconventional part of Jack's system. It's his remote control boat anchor that sets him apart from the crowd. Jack parks his boat where he wants to start fishing, wades downstream, and when he wants to move, raises the anchor with a remote control and lets his boat float downstream to him. No sloshing back upstream to get the boat. No worries about rising water.

Jack has also developed a fly and a technique to fish it that has accounted for uncountable catches. The fly, named for it's thin waist and fat thorax, is called the Dirt Dauber. The actual dirt dauber is a member of the wasp family.

Interview:

Q: How long have you fished the Little Red River?
A: I've fished the Red River for 12 years.

Q: How long have you trout fished?
A: I've been fly fishing the Little Red River for 10 years.

Q: What did you do in your non-fishing life?
A: I owned a home improvement business in Helena, Ark.

Q: Have you fly fished for other fish than trout?
A: No.

Q: What do you look for in selecting a piece of water to fish?
A: The first thing that I look for is privacy. That's getting tougher all the time. My favorite water is fast, with a broken surface and between 18 to 30 inches deep.

Q: Do you primarily wade or boat fish?
A: I wade. I use my boat to get to places that I like to wade.

Q: Do you use a wading staff?
A: No. Falling really isn't a concern with my float tube.

Q: Who has influenced your fishing and how?
A: Two of my close friends, Rick Rasnick, and the late Jimmy Stewart. (Note: Rick Rasnick is featured in this publication.)

Q: What times of day do you primarily fish?
A: I like early morning the best. I like to start before boat traffic is moving and the shoals start to fill up with people.

Q: Do you fish high water?
A: No. I prefer to wade.

Q: What are your favorite flies?
A: My favorite fly is the Dirt Dauber.

Q: How do you fish them?
A: Almost always on the bottom.

Q: Do you use any special leaders or rigs for your favorite flies?
A: I like to use a 10-foot leader with a 2-foot tippet. I'll usually put my weight 2 feet above my fly and my indicator 6 feet above my weight. I generally use quite a bit of weight with this rig.

Q: Do you use strike indicators? What kind?
A: I generally make my own indicators from double sided foam tape. I'll taper the end toward the fly. I want the indicator to pull my fly downstream.

Q: What size fly do you fish most often?
A: I use a Size 14 Dirt Dauber the most often. Every now and then I'll move up to a Size 12 or down to a Size 16.

Q: Does fly color matter?
A: I think that fly color is important. I like to use a fly with contrast. The Dirt Dauber has a dark thorax and a light abdomen, or the other way around.

Q: Do you use fluorocarbon?
A: I generally use Seguar Fluorocarbon tippets.

Q: Does your leader change with different flies?
A: Yes, when I midge fish I'll use lighter tippets and less weight below the indicator.

Q: What kind of knots do you use.
A: I'll use the Orvis knot for tying the fly to the hook and a double surgeons knot to connect sections of line.

Q: What is your favorite piece of equipment?
A: That's easy; my remote control anchor.

Q: What tips or advice would you give a first-time fisherman on the Red River?
A: Fish twice as deep and use twice as much weight as you think that you should.

Q: What's your favorite rod, reel and line combination?
A: Rod – Orvis T3, 3-weight
   Reel – Orvis Mid Arbor.
   Line – Scientific Angler's weight forward.

Q: Do you tie your own flies?
A: Yes, I tie all of the flies that I fish.

Q: Do you design your own flies?
A: The Dirt Dauber is a fly that I designed.

Q: What about bead heads?
A: I don't use many bead heads except on midges.

Q: How do the seasons affect your fishing.
A: Actually, they don't have any effect at all.

Q: Does your fly selection change with water type or seasonally?
A: Yes, my neon Dirt Dauber is a hatch breaker in the spring and fall during caddis hatching. (Tied with bright colors of ice dubbing for a body and a wing and tail of Antron yarn.) I also like a La Fontaine Sparkle Pupa for caddis.

Q: Does your favorite river access change with the seasons?
A: Not at all.

Q: How does the time of day affect your fishing?
A: First light is the best. Especially during the spawn. I like to be the first to fish any spot.

Q: Do you prefer rising, falling or stable water?
A: My first choice would be dead low water. Next, I'd like falling water. I don't like fresh rising water.

Q: Are fish signs important to your style of fishing?
A: In the past I never really focused on them. Now, however, since I started fishing midges, they are very important. Now I look for rising fish.

Q: What is your favorite fishing technique? (Swing, strip or dead drift.)
A: I like to cast upstream with my indicator dragging my fly downstream along the bottom. This is how I fish my Dirt Dauber, which is designed to ride hook up and is almost weedless.

Q: What has been the biggest change you have seen on the Little Red River?
A: There is a lot more pressure on the lower river and I'm constantly irritated by people keeping fish.

Q: Do you ever night fish?
A: Never.

Q: What changes do you or don't care for?
A: Well obviously I hate to see the increased fishing pressure. I think that the fishery has declined over time with respect to the size of the rainbow trout. I haven't noticed the same thing with the brown trout. I think that they are doing fine.

Dirt Dauber

Originated by Jack Kirby
Tied by Jack Kirby

Hook – Mustad 3399 Size 12-14
Thread – 8/0 black
Weight – 10 – 12 wraps .015 lead wire wrapped at the bend of the hook. (This makes the fly ride in a hook up position.)
Abdomen – Dark hare's ear. Dubbed loose.
Thoax - Light Sow Scud dubbing
Wing Case (Area directly behind the head) – Dark hare's ear
Legs – Mallard flank feather fibers
Head – Tying thread.

Phil Landry

Don't get all caught up in the hype of the spawn; stay away from it.

Phil Landry is a self-taught fly fisherman. He traded a traditional teaching career for a classroom on the river.

Phil learned to fish when he was just 10 years old in Colorado. While in college he started guiding in Guadalupe, for bass. In 2000, he graduated with a Masters Degree in Education from the University of Texas, Austin. Phil taught briefly after graduation and worked for a while at Bass Pro.

From there, Phil worked for Outdoor Inc. in Memphis. Phil gradually moved into working as a fishing guide on the Little Red River. He has been a guide on the Little Red full time for the last five years. He books more than 100 trips a year.

Phil decided to work as a guide while in college working at a summer camp. He decided to take the two things that he loved the most; working outside and teaching, mix them and make them into a career.

Phil's knowledge of the river is excellent: He knows where to find fish. He also places a priority on ensuring his clients have a good time.

Interview:

Q: How long have you fished the Red River?
A: Since Spring '93.

Q: How long have you trout fished?
A: Seriously, Spring '93.

Q: What did you, or do you, do in your non-fishing life?
A: I don't think that I've had a non-fishing life.

Q: Have you fly fished for other fish than trout?
A: I have fished for redfish, bonefish, snook, tarpon, permit, Atlantic salmon, stripers and bass.

Q: How has this influenced your trout fishing?
A: It has made me a better caster as well as a more versatile streamer fisherman.

Q: What do you look for in selecting a piece of water to fish?
A: I look for tailouts, seams, structure, borders, and transition areas — (deep-to-shallow and weed-to-clear areas.)

Q: Who has influenced your fishing and how?
A: Jeff Hawthorne has been a friendly and patient teacher. The most important thing that Jeff taught me was how to pick the water that I am going to fish with respect to the water level. Jack Kirby taught me a lot of spots to fish in the lower river. (Note: These two fishermen are also featured in this publication.)

Q: Do you primarily wade or boat fish?
A: I think that I fish 80% of the time in a boat and 20% of the time wading.

Q: Do you use a wading staff?
A: No.

Q: What times of day do you primarily fish?
A: In the spring and the fall I like to fish mid morning. In the winter I like to fish in the afternoon the best. In the summer I'd pick the early morning.

Q: Do you fish high water?
A: Yes. Big flies and heavy lines are the keys. I use 200-grain, 24-foot sink tips.

Q: What are your favorite flies?
A: Sowbugs. On one unit of water—big streamers.

Q: How do you fish them?
A: I like to dead drift nymphs. I'll strip big streamers.

Q: What size fly do you fish most often?
A: Either Size 14 or 16.

Q: Does fly color matter?

A: Absolutely. Color is one of the three big triggers. They are profile, size and color, in that order.

Q: Do you use any special leaders or rigs for your favorite flies?
A: I don't use a lot of specialized leaders, but I like fishing droppers a lot. I'll normally fish two flies. For example; I'll fish a caddis larva under a dry fly.

Q: Does your leader change with different flies?
A: Not much. For nymphs, I like a 9-foot, 5X leader with a dropper. When I use streamers, I'll use a 4.5-foot, 2X piece of fluorocarbon for a tippet.

Q: Do you use fluorocarbon?
A: Usually, but it's not needed in dirty water. I try to avoid big pieces of fluorocarbon and I'm careful with loose pieces, because fluorocarbon will not degrade in the environment.

Q: Do you use strike indicators? What kind?
A: Yes. I use Palsa stick on indicators with clients and beginners. They are easy to apply, and they stay in place. For my own fishing I usually prefer to use yarn indicators.

Q: What kind of knots do you use.
A: This is really simple. Use the knots that you know and can tie the best. These are the knots that I use:
- Fly to tippet – Improved cinch.
- Tippet to leader – Triple surgeons.
- Leader to fly line – Nail knot.
- Fly line to backing – Perfection loop.

Q: What is your favorite piece of equipment?
A: My boat. I really love to row.

Q: What tips or advice would you give a first time fisherman on the Little Red River?

A: Don't get all caught up in the hype of the spawn; stay away from it.

Q: What's your favorite rod, reel and line combination?
A: My favorite setup is a 9-foot, 3-weight, Sage XP with a Ross Evolution and a 4-weight Rio nymph line.

Q: Do you tie your own flies?
A: Yes, always.

Q: Do you design your own flies?
A: I design new patterns all the time.

Q: What about bead heads?
A: I use them on dropper rigs. I think that their effectiveness is due to their extra weight that they give a fly.

Q: How do the seasons affect your fishing.
A: Seasonal variations have a big effect on how the fish move in the river. For example, there is a 15-day period that red horse suckers spawn in the lower river, and browns just stack up just below them.

Q: Does your fly selection change with water type or seasonally?
A: I'll typically fish smaller flies in the winter. (Size 18 to 16 sowbugs)

Q: Does your favorite river access change with the seasons?
A: My favorite access point will change based on daily water flow variations more so than the seasons. Dripping Springs is my favorite access because it provides the greatest range of water: You can fish water from Lobo all the way to Ramsey. That being said, I think that spring is my favorite season.

Q: How does the time of day affect your fishing?
A: Normally the water level is tied to the time of day.

Q: Do you prefer rising, falling or stable water?
A: Slowly falling water in the summer is hard to beat.

Q: Are fish signs important to your style of fishing?
A: I know where fish hold. I usually fish the water.

Q: What is your favorite fishing technique? (Swing, strip or dead drift.)
A: Stripping large articulated streamers is my all-time favorite method of fishing.

Q: What has been the biggest change you have seen on the Little Red River?
A: In the mid 90's there was a big increase in fishing pressure. The record fish and the movie really pushed it.

Another change on the river is that jet boat use is much more popular, and this has really opened up the river. There used to be areas that just didn't get much traffic.

Q: What changes do you or don't care for?
A: The increase of fishing pressure and the promotion of the brown trout spawn.

Q: Do you ever night fish?
A: I used to night fish a lot, but it really interferes with guiding.

Articulated Streamer

Tied by Phil Landry

Trailer
Hook – Mustad – 9672 Size 6
Thread – 8/0 black
Head – ¼" Foam popper head reversed
Tail – Black rabbit strip
Body – Black Cactus Chenile

Main Fly
Hook – Mustad 9674 Size 4
Thread – 8/0 black
Connector Loop – 20 Lb. Mono
Eyes – Lead dumbbell 1/8"
Tail – Black marabou
Body – Black Cactus Chenile
Wing – Black rabbit strip
Legs – Clear and black Barred Crazy Legs
Head – Black Cactus Chenile

Rick Rasnick

I was raised in a hunting and fishing environment. My father had the greatest influence on me, because he taught me to appreciate nature and the outdoors.

Rick Rasnick is one of the finest midge fisherman in the Red River area.

Most of his fishing is sight based. Rasnick, a retired Army Lieutenant Colonel, has learned through careful observation and patience, where fish hold, how they feed, and how to present his fly. Rick's casts are short. His tippets are light. His flies are small: Tiny actually. Often, he modifies his rig or drift to watch how the fish react to his presentation. Rick actually improves each time he fishes.

Midge fishing on the Little Red, he says, is worth learning because midges hatch every day on the Little Red, so they are constantly available to the fish. Good midge presentations rarely spook fish. Although, Rick generally likes to move around, he's been known to take as many as 20 fish, sometimes more, without moving his feet.

Casting Buggers through the pool will also take some fish, Rasnick says, but the commotion of casting a much bigger fly seems to put the fish down pretty quick. Midge fishing, with its tiny flies works well in pressured water: There's less disturbance; less alarm to the fish. "Relaxed fish feed; stressed fish hide," he says.

Watching Rick, one might think that he has a secret fly, a special rig, or a trick presentation. While he may have all of these, none are the secret to his success. His real secret is the detailed observation, in-depth study, and natural understanding of his prey: The results of 10-years of accumulated experience spent on the water simply paying attention to what the fish are doing in the current.

Rick once landed a 26-inch rainbow trout just below the Swinging Bridge Resort. Rasnick, wading at the time, landed the fish on a 7X tippet and a Size 22 fly.

Interview:

Q: How long have you trout fished on the Little Red River?
A: Ten years.

Q: How long have you trout fished?
A: Ten years.

Q: What did you do in your non-fishing life?
A: I spent 20 years in the U.S. Army, retiring as a Lieutenant Colonel.

Q: Have you fly fished for fish other than trout?
A: When I was in Texas, I fished for both bass and bream.

Q: Has fishing for other fish, influenced your trout fishing?
A: No.

Q: What do you look for in selecting a piece of water to fish?
A: I like to fish a depth of 2- to 3-feet the best. I look for different or changing bottom characteristics such as terraces, holes or pockets.

Q: Who has influenced your trout fishing?
A: My father had the greatest influence, because he taught me to appreciate nature and the outdoors. I was raised in a hunting and fishing environment. Another influence was Dave Whitlock. His book, <u>A Guide to Aquatic Trout Food</u>, and his innovative tying style, have improved my trout fishing.

Q: Do you prefer to wade or boat fish?
A: Wading suits my style of fishing better than boat fishing. Controlling the drift is much easier wading than from a boat.

Q: Do you use a wading staff?
A: Always, I think that a wading staff is really important. It has saved me from some nasty falls.

Q: What times of day do you primarily fish?
A: My favorite time is between noon and 3 p.m. Normally there aren't great hatches of midges early in the morning.

Q: Do you fish high water?
A: No, actually almost all of my fishing is wading.

Q: What are your favorite flies?
A: Midges and nymphs. My particular favorites are Yong Specials, Pupae imitations, Pheasant tails, RS-2s and Baetis nymphs.

Q: How do you fish them?
A: Usually I'll drift them under an indicator.

Q: Does fly color matter?
A: Generally I prefer a darker fly. I also like to have some contrast between the thorax and the abdomen of the fly, with the thorax, the darker of the two. When I fish midges I usually prefer brown.

Q: Do you use any special leaders or rigs for your favorite flies?
A: The leader that I use most often is a 9-foot Rio, 5X leader which I build to twelve feet long. In especially flat (calm) water I may use a 15-foot leader, and then in exceptionally fast water I may trim down to 7.5 feet.

Q: Does your leader change with different flies?
A: Yes, for flies that are smaller than Size 16, I generally use a 7X tippet. For flies that are Size 16 to 18, I use 6X tippets. The depth that you present your fly is as important as the fly type. I generally start with my fly 24-28 inches below my indicator. The depth you fish can be controlled by mending your line. I will usually

mend differently or add weight to my leader before I move my indicator up or down. Generally if I'm not getting hits, I fish deeper.

Q: Do you use fluorocarbon?
A: Yes and I use 7X the most often.

Q: Do you use strike indicators? If so, what kind?
A: I generally use one half of a white Palsa stick-on indicator.

Q: What size fly do you fish most often?
A: Size 20 and 22.

Q: What kind of knots do you use?
A: To connect sections of a leader I use a double surgeon's knot. For flies I use a Eugene Bend for emergers and a double surgeons knot for nymphs.

Q: What is your favorite piece of equipment?
A: My lanyard. The things that I need the most are right at hand. No fumbling with vest pockets or a pack. If I were to pick a second piece of equipment, I have to say my wading staff.

Q: What tips or advice would you give to a first time fisherman on the Little Red River?
A: Read some books to get the basics. One of my favorites is Dave Whitlock's <u>Guide to Aquatic Trout Food</u>.

Q: What is your favorite rod and reel combination?
  Rod – Winston 9-foot, 4-weight WT
  Reel - Abel TR1
  Line – Rio Double Taper Selective Floating

Q: Do you tie your own flies?
A: Yes. It would be unusual for me to fish a fly that was purchased or tied by someone else.

Q: Do you design your own flies?
A: Yes, in a sense. I usually modify existing patterns.

Q: What about bead heads?
A: I use bead heads quite a bit on size 20-24 patterns. Nickel colored beads are my favorite. I use them in windy or murky colored water conditions.

Q: How does the season affect your fishing?
A: Other than using smaller patterns during the winter, the seasons do not really have much of an effect on my fishing. I tend to use more emerger patterns during the summer.

Q: Does your river access point change with the seasons?
A: In the fall I like to fish Cow Shoals. In the heat of the summer, I rarely fish JFK (the park at the dam site.)

Q: How does time of day affect your fishing?
A: I like to start fishing around noon. Most people are leaving for lunch about then, and insect activity doesn't really begin until mid-day. I also believe that my best big fish opportunity is between 1 and 3 pm.

Q: Do you prefer rising, falling or stable water?
A: I prefer falling water, but I still want a fishable current. I really don't like to fish dead water.

Q: Are fish signs important to your style of fishing?
A: Fish signs are definitely important. They will tell you more than the fish are just there. They will tell you if fish are aggressively feeding or just holding. Proposing fish indicate that they are feeding on midge pupas. Flashing fish are aggressively feeding subsurface.

Q: What is your favorite fishing technique? (Swing, strip or dead drift)
A: Drifting under an indicator is my favorite technique, but I sure wouldn't call it dead drifting. Line manage-

ment, mending and slack line casting all affect your drift. For example, a down stream mend will force your fly to move faster than the current.

Q: What has been the biggest change you have seen on the Little Red River?
A: There have been two. The increased development has degraded the water quality, and the fishing pressure has increased tremendously.

Q: What changes do you or don't care for?
A: I'm concerned about the spread of the Didymo algae. I'm not sure anyone understands the long-term effects of this with regard to the trout and insect habitat.

On a positive note, I like the habitat improvement at Winkley Shoals.

Q: Do you ever night fish?
A: No, I prefer to sight fish.

RS2

Originated by Rim Chung
Tied by Rick Rasnick

Hook – Tiemco 100BL Size 20
Thread – 8/0 Black
Tail – Blue dun Micro Fibbetts
Body – Olive antron dubbing
Wing – CDC feather, trimmed
Head – Tying thread

Yong Special

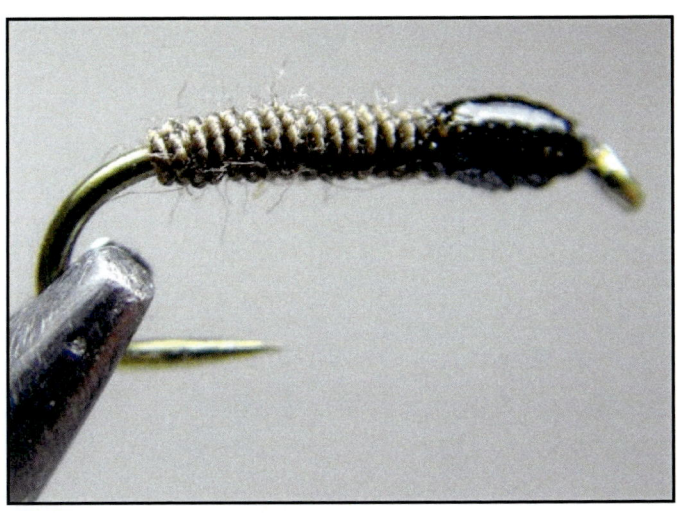

Originated by Andy Kim
Tied by Rick Rasnick

Hook – Tiemco 100BL Size 20
Thread – 8/0 Black
Body – Coats and Clark Summer Brown All Purpose
Head –Tying thread, Note – Build up a buky thread head

M1

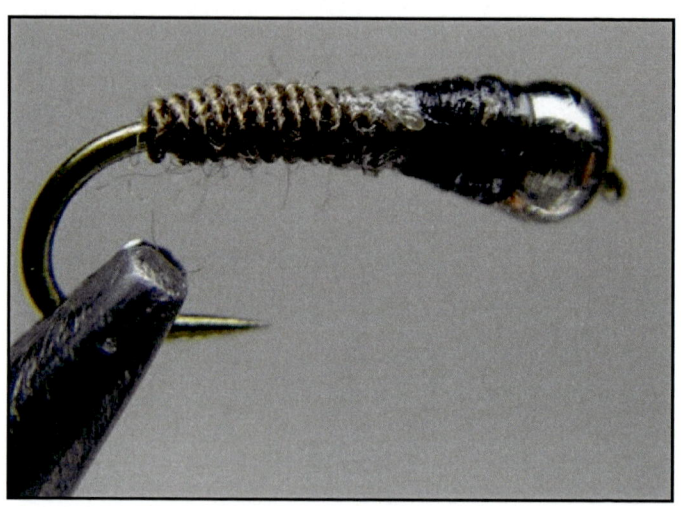

Originated by Rick Rasnick
Tied by Rick Rasnick

Hook – Tiemco 100BL
Thread – 8/0 black
Bead – Nickle Bead (1/16th for Size 22 fly, 5/64" for Size 20 fly)
Body – Coats and Clark Summer Brown All Purpose
Collar – Tying thread

Jamie Rouse

I'm not sure that I have a non-fishing life as an adult. When I haven't been fishing, I've been guiding.

Jamie Rouse's depth of knowledge, range of experience and, most of all, his enthusiasm for fishing in all its forms is impressive and contagious.

He may be the busiest and hardest-working guide in the area. He is currently an Orvis Endorsed Guide and won their prestigious Guide of the Year award for 2007. He guided fishermen in Alaska for 14 years, working for the Rainbow King Lodge.

Jamie has fished for freshwater and saltwater species all over North America, and blended these techniques into his own unique style of fishing.

He is one of those guides who won't shy away from a challenge. Jamie led the way in pioneering successful ways of fishing the relentless high water conditions of 2008. And he caught a lot fish, too.

He's not one of your "let's drift a sowbug under an indicator all day," kind of guides. Jamie guides for other species than trout including smallmouth, hybrids and even carp.

Interview:

Q: How long have you fished the Little Red River?
A: I've fished the Little Red River for 35 years. I have been a guide on the Little Red for 14 years. I've lived here for the last 7 years.

Q: How long have you trout fished?
A: I've fished for trout for 35 years.

Q: What did you or do you do in your non-fishing life?
A: I'm not sure that I have a non-fishing life as an adult. When I haven't been fishing; I've been guiding.

Q: Have you fly fished for other fish than trout?
A: Yes, I've fished for salmon, char, tarpon, roosterfish, bonefish, permit, striped bass, hybrid bass, smallmouth bass, largemouth bass and carp.

Q: How has this influenced your trout fishing?
A: This has mainly influenced how I streamer fish. I frequently use lead core and intermediate lines.

Q: What do you look for in selecting water to fish?
A: I just love tailouts. But I really like to experiment.

Q: Who has influenced your fishing and how?
A: Dale Fulton. I worked for Dale for a year, when I was 22 and thought that I knew everything. I think that the most important thing he taught me was patience.

Q: Do you primarily wade or boat fish?
A: I really like to do both.

Q: Do you use a wading staff?
A: No, not yet.

Q: What times of day do you primarily fish?
A: If I'm big fish hunting, my favorite time is around 4 a.m. My next favorite time would be twilight.

Q: Do you fish high water?
A: I fish high water frequently. When fishing high water, use a lot of weight. I don't always use an indicator because it limits the depth. Avoid the usual low-water spots; fish inside turns and below eddies, not in them.

Q: What are your favorite flies?
A: I like a Hare's Ear, small jigs, and now and then some caddis drys and emergers, but I really like to fish streamers the best.

Q: How do you fish them?
A: I don't drift steamers much; I actively strip them.

Q: Does fly color matter?
A: Color definitely matters, but not as much as profile, size and movement: In that order.

Q: Do you use any special leaders or rigs for your favorite flies?
A: Of course. I think that really long leaders are much more effective. They enable you to fish much farther away from the line disturbance caused from casting and stripping.

Q: Does your leader change with different flies?
A: Yes. I use intermediate full sink lines and 30-feet of a lead core line for a fly line when I fish streamers. I have found that the middle section of old trout leaders works very well as a leader with these lines.

Q: Do you use fluorocarbon?
A: Yes, my favorite is Mirage. I don't usually use fluorocarbon when I streamer fish, unless the water is exceptionally clear.

Q: What kind of knots do you use?
A: I use a Duncan loop for my fly connections and a regular Duncan knot for line to line connections.

Q: Do you use strike indicators? What kind?
A: I use the smallest and the lightest that I can. I think Palsa indicators are the ones that I use the most. I usually use white, and when I fish at Bull Shoals I'll often use half of a white Palsa indicator.

Q: What size fly do you fish most often?
A: When I fish for myself, I'll pick a Size 6 streamer.

Q: What is your favorite piece of equipment?
A: My 9-foot, Salty Six T-3. It's my favorite rod.

Q: What tips or advice would you give a first time fisherman on the Little Red River?
A: Don't be lulled into thinking that every time you lift your rod to set your hook it's another cookie cutter rainbow. It may just be a monster fish. I have seen this happen over and over.

Q: What's your favorite rod, reel and line combination?
A: I like my 9-foot Salty Six rod with 30-feet of 200-grain lead core line and good mid-arbor reel.

Q: Do you tie your own flies?
A: Yes, I still tie most of the flies that I fish with.

Q: Do you design your own flies?
A: I design quite a few flies. Two that I fish often are the Red Diablo (a soft hackle,) and the AC Sowbug.

Q: What about bead heads?
A: I fish bead heads all the time. My philosophy is that if it's legal, and doesn't hurt the fish, the technique is fair game.

Q: How do the seasons affect your fishing?
A: The seasons really do influence my fishing. I like fishing dry flies in the spring (March browns.) And I like fishing terrestrials in the summer (beetles and hoppers.) Fall might be my favorite time on the river because it is so pretty. I don't fish bedding browns.

Q: Does your fly selection change with water type or seasonally?
A: In the spring I'll dry fly fish. The rest of the year, except for late summer, most of my presentations are subsurface.

Q: Does your favorite river access change with the seasons?
A: The access will change more with water conditions and generation schedules than the season. My favorite access with high water conditions is Lobo.

Q: How does the time of day affect your fishing?
A: I like to fish low light conditions for browns especially during low water conditions or times when there is an abnormal amount of fishing pressure on the river.

Q: Do you prefer rising, falling or stable water?
A: I like falling water the best. Usually, falling water means a lot of fish.

Q: Are fish signs important to your style of fishing?
A: Typically, I fish the water. If I'm fishing drys or emergers, fish signs like rising fish are more important to me. The signs of active big fish are extremely important.

Q: What is your favorite fishing technique? (Swing, strip or dead drift.)
A: Without a doubt, stripping big streamers.

Q: What has been the biggest change you have seen on the Little Red River?
A: Since I have been guiding I have really noticed that the increased development on the river has adversely affected water quality.

Q: What changes do you or don't care for?
A: Well, obviously, the tremendous increase in development on the river.

Q: Do you ever night fish?
A: Absolutely. I love it.

Red Diablo

Originated by Jamie Rouse
Tied by Jamie Rouse

Hook – Orvis 2457 Sizes 16-12
Head – Glass bead
Thread – 8/0 red
Weight – 10 wraps .015" lead wire substitute
Body – Red SLF dubbing
Rib – Red copper wire
Collar – Hungarian partridge with filoplume in a dubbing loop to make the wing case

Ron Burgandy

Originated by Jamie Rouse
Tied by Jamie Rouse

Hook – Gamakatsu Stinger hook Size 6
Thread – 6/0 red
Eyes – Bead chain
Tail – ¼" Natural brown rabbit strip. Note – tie a mono loop under the tail to keep the tail from fouling around the hook.
Body – Palmer the rabbit strip used for the tail.
Collar – Tan ginger marabou
Head – Brown fur or dubbing, dubbed and wrapped around the bead chain eyes.

AC Sowbug

Originated by Jamie Rouse
Tied by Jamie Rouse

Hook – Orvis 1641 Sizes 16-14
Thread – 6/0 white
Tail – White thread
Weight – Size 12 fly - .030" lead wire substitute, Size 14 fly - .025" lead wire substitute, Size 16 Fly - .020" lead wire substitute
Body – Tan Sow Scud dubbing
Shellback – Brown Thin Skin trimmed to proper width
Note – Immediately after dubbing flatten the fly with a pliers.

Bob Silzer

Don't get stuck thinking that a sowbug and an indicator is the only way to fish here. Experiment! Lot's of techniques work. Develop your own style.

Bob Silzer is one of the best all-around fly fisherman on the River.

Bob was born in northeast Pennsylvania in 1962. He currently works as a neurologist at Little Rock Diagnostic Clinic. Bob got an early start fishing with his dad, who was a tournament bass fisherman. Bob and his father frequently fished for bass and bream in ponds.

Bob started fly fishing about 10 years ago at McCleland's on the White River. He has since fly fished in the Gulf of Mexico, Kamchatka, Ukraine, and Alaska. While most of his fly fishing is on the Little Red River, Bob's home waters include Sylamore Creek, the Buffalo, the Norfork, and White rivers.

Interview

Q: How long have you fished the Little Red River?
A: For 10 years.

Q: How long have you trout fished?
A: For 13 years. I have fly fished for the last 10 years.

Q: What do you do in your non-fishing life?
A: I'm a doctor.

Q: Have you fly fished for other fish than trout?
A: Yes, I've fished for redfish, specks, pompano, spanish mackerel, smallies, bream, largemouth, hybrids, carp and drum.

Q: How has this influenced your trout fishing?
A: I have learned how to use different flies, improved my ability to read water and it has certainly made me a better caster.

Q: What do you look for in selecting a piece of water to fish?
A: Fast water slowing down as the depth drops off, tailouts, and rising fish.

Q: Who has influenced your fishing and how?
A: Bill Willmert has influenced my casting, fishing of streamers, and taught me various retrieves. Rick Rasnick has taught me a lot about midge fishing. Ben Wiedower has shown me a lot of patterns. (Editor's Note: These three fishermen are also featured in this publication.)

Q: Do you primarily wade or boat fish?
A: Usually I like to wade.

Q: Do you use a wading staff?
A: No.

Q: What times of day do you primarily fish?
A: I usually fish all day. I prefer fishing from mid-afternoon to dark.

Q: Do you fish high water?
A: Not very much. I really don't like it. High water limits the places that you can fish. When I do fish high water, I fish streamers or a Red Ass dropped off of an egg.

Q: What are your favorite flies?
A: My two favorites are a Leech, (similar to a Woolly Bugger except the body hackle is replaced by a mallard flank feather tied in like a soft hackle), either tied in olive or olive and black in a Size 12, and a brown Crackleback in a Size 16 or 18.

Q: How do you fish them?
A: Stripping.

Q: Does fly color matter?
A: Yes, at certain times of year.

Q: Do you use any special leaders or rigs for your favorite flies?
A: Not really. For stripping flies I use an 11- or 12-foot, 5X leader. I rarely use a 6X or 7X tippet.

Q: Does your leader change with different flies?
A: No.

Q: Do you use fluorocarbon?
A: I use fluorocarbon for tippets only.

Q: Do you use strike indicators? What kind?
A: I like Palsa and Lightning Strike foam, stick-on indicators. Lightning Strike indicators do not leave residue on your line.

Q: What size fly do you fish most often?
A: Size 12 for my Leech and Size 18 for Cracklebacks.

Q: What kind of knots do you use?
A: Line to leader – nail knot
Tippet to leader – double surgeons knot
Tippet to fly – improved cinch knot

Q: What is your favorite piece of equipment?
A: My favorite rod is a Winston, 8-foot 9-inch, 5-weight LT.

Q: What tips or advice would you give a first time fisherman on the Little Red River?
A: Don't get stuck thinking that a sowbug and an indicator is the only way to fish here. Experiment! Lot's of techniques work. Develop your own style.

Q: What's your favorite rod, reel and line combination?
A: Along with my Winston rod I like a Galvan Torque or a Ross Evolution reel and a 5-weight GPX, weight forward, floating line.

Q: Do you tie your own flies?
A: Yes.

Q: Do you design your own flies?
A: I modify existing flies. My Leech, brown Crackleback and CDC Emerger are examples of flies that I modified and fish all the time.

Q: What about bead heads?
A: I have gotten away from the use of bead heads. I use them sometimes on midges. I just don't like them much.

Q: How do the seasons affect your fishing.
A: I like to fish for browns in the fall, and I also enjoy fishing the caddis hatches in the early spring.

Q: Does your fly selection change with water type or seasonally?
A: For pre-spawning browns in pools, I like my brown Size 16 Crackleback. For spawning browns on shoals, I use an egg with an orange ass soft hackle dropper. The Leech works all year long.

Q: Does your favorite river access change with the seasons?
A: I fish Cow Shoals and below the Swinging Bridge in the fall. I like to fish Mossy Shoal in the spring during the caddis hatch. In the winter I fish JFK (Park.)

Q: How does the time of day affect your fishing?
A: Early in the morning I'll start with a streamer. As the day wears on I'll go smaller and smaller.

Q: Do you prefer rising, falling or stable water?
A: Stable.

Q: Are fish signs important to your style of fishing?
A: Definitely. Fish signs are very important. Rises tell you that fish are around and feeding.

Q: What is your favorite fishing technique? (Swing, strip or dead drift.)
A: Swinging.

Q: What has been the biggest change you have seen on the Little Red River?

A: The increase of fishing pressure on the river.

Q: What changes do you or don't care for?
A: Again the pressure and the continued development. People don't respect or honor the water. I frequently see more and more litter and the mishandling of fish.

Q: Do you ever night fish?
A: Rarely.

Brown Crackleback

Originated by Bob Story
Tied by Bob Silzer

Hook – Tiemco 100 Size 18
Thread 8/0 brown
Shellback – Peacock herl
Body – Brown Awesome Possum Dubbing
Head – Tying thread

CDC RS Emerger

Originated by Bob Silzer
Tied by Bob Silzer

Hook – Tiemco 100 Size 18
Thread – 8/0 olive
Rib – Two strands of silver wire
Tail - Pearl Krystal Flash
Body – Tan rabbit fur
Wing – Natural CDC
Head – Tying thread

Leech

Tied by Bob Silzer

Hook – Mustad 9672 Size 12
Thread – 8/0 olive
Weight – Ten wraps .015 lead wire,
Tail – Mixed olive, yellow, and black marabou
Flash – Silver Krystal Flash
Body – Olive Awesome Possum Dubbing
Head – Tying thread

Ben Wiedower

I try to find water with fish. Fish signs —rising or actively feeding fish—are very important.

Ben Wiedower was born in Guy, Ark. in 1945. Ben worked as an electrician, the Chief Building Inspector in Conway, Ark., and a private contractor.

He built a second home on Cow Shoals, on the Little Red River, and began fly fishing in 2002, He worked hard, covered a lot of water and now spends over 100 days a year on the river. Ben has often fished with other guides, some featured in this publication, including John Wilson, Chuck Farneth, Eb Estes, Donnie Hyslip, and Bill Willmert. He also fishes regularly with Rick Rasnick and Bob Silzer. He largely credits this group for his early success.

Ben excels as a fisherman because of his exhausting work ethic and versatility on the water. Ben's feet never "grow into the river bottom" and Ben will move, change rigs, flies and presentations until he finds fish and establishes what bass fishermen would call a pattern.

Ben comes as close as anyone to applying a systematic approach to catching fish. He calls the Little Red, Table Rock, the White and the Little Missouri Rivers his home waters.

Interview:

Q: How long have you fished the Red River?
A: Seven Years.

Q: How long have you trout fished?
A: Seven years.

Q: What did you do in your non-fishing life?
A: I've spent most of my career in the electrical business and in contracting.

Q: Have you fly fished for other fish than trout?
A: I've fished for char, salmon and rainbows in Kamchatka, Ukraine, and Alaska.

Q: Has this influenced your trout fishing?
A: I don't think so.

Q: What do you look for in selecting a piece of water to fish?
A: I try to find water with fish. Fish signs, (rising or actively feeding fish) are important keys to locating catchable fish. I'll normally start with a Deena as a searching pattern. If there are no takers I'll either fish with a nymph and a midge dropper or simply midge fish. If there are still no fish I'll move and start the process again. I think that knee deep water with a current and lots of rocks is some of my favorite water.

Q: Who has influenced your fishing and how?
A: Bill Willmert, Rick Rasnick, Chuck Farneth, and Bob Silzer. I fished often with these people and all of them have shared spots, flies and techniques with me. (These four fishermen are also featured in this publication.)

Q: Do you primarily wade or boat fish?
A: I prefer to wade.

Q: Do you use a wading staff?
A: Yes, I've carried one for the last three years. I use it getting to the water and then again when I'm wading in unknown water.

Q: What times of day do you primarily fish?
A: I think that I like early morning best, around sun up.

Q: Do you fish high water?
A: Not very well.

Q: What are your favorite flies?
A: Deena, midge pupae – Either a Yong Special or a Zebra Midge. In the fall I like a Red Ass dropped off of an egg pattern, (where permitted) and sowbugs.

Q: How do you fish them?
A: I dead drift midges; I strip Deenas.

Q: Does fly color matter?
A: I think so. I usually prefer darker colors.

Q: Do you use any special leaders or rigs for your favorite flies?
A: No, not at all. I normally use a 9-foot, 5X leader with a 4-foot tippet to start. (2- feet of 5X and 2-feet of 6X tippet.) For dead drifting I'll use either a 6X or 7X tippet. For stripping I usually use a 5X tippet.

Q: Does your leader change with different flies?
A: I will change my tippet, not my leader.

Q: Do you use fluorocarbon?
A: Yes, always. Well I didn't in Russia, but here I do.

Q: Do you use strike indicators? What kind?
A: Yes. I like Palsa stick on indicators the best. I think white indicators annoy the fish the least. Fish are used to seeing white things float by. Bits of foam and bubbles.

Q: What size fly do you fish most often?
A: Size 18 or 20.

Q: What kind of knots do you use.
A: Tippet to leader – double surgeons knot
   Tippet to fly – for large flies – Eugene Bend
   For small flies – double surgeon's knot

Q: What is your favorite piece of equipment?
A: My Sage 9-foot, 5-weight Z-axis fly rod.

Q: What tips or advice would you give a first time fisherman on the Red River?
A: Stop and look for fish signs. Fish small flies, Size 18 or smaller

Q: What's your favorite rod, reel and line combination?
A: Along with my 5-weight Z-Axis rod, I like an Orvis

Bar stock, mid-arbor reel or my Galvan Torque reel. My favorite fly line is a 5-weight SA shark skin. I really like the way this line casts.

Q: Do you tie your own flies?
A: Yes.

Q: Do you design your own flies?
A: No, I use established Little Red patterns.

Q: What about bead heads?
A: I use a lot of bead heads. I prefer the silver ones. I have a bead head egg pattern that I catch quite a few fish on. I'll use bead heads on most of my nymph patterns, and I fish a lot of droppers, where I use bead heads most of the time.

Q: How do the seasons affect your fishing.
A: I'll change my approach as the seasons change. For example: In the fall I tend to use more soft hackles, in the summer I use more midges, and in the spring, I'll also use mostly midges. In April, I start to look for caddis hatches down river.

Q: Does your fly selection change with water type or seasonally?
A: In off-color water I use bigger and brighter flies. I use micro-jigs frequently, in dingy water.

Q: Does your favorite river access change with the seasons?
A: I like to fish Cow Shoals in the fall and Mossy in the summer.

Q: How does the time of day affect your fishing?
A: Early in the morning I'll start with a Deena or soft hackles. Then I'll switch to midges. In the late afternoon I start fishing with the Deena again, and when the action slows, switch to midges again.

Q: Do you prefer rising, falling or stable water?
A: Stable or falling.

Q: Are fish signs important to your style of fishing?
A: Yes, they tell me where the fish are.

Q: What is your favorite fishing technique? (Swing, strip or dead drift.)
A: Dead drifting.

Q: What has been the biggest change you have seen on the Little Red River?
A: I consider myself a short timer in terms of the time that I have fished the river. That being said, I have seen an increase in pressure since I have been fishing the river.

Q: What changes do you or don't care for?
A: I think that the growing pressure on the river has hurt the fishing.

Q: Do you ever night fish?
A: No.

Zebra Midge

Tied by Bill Willmert

Hook – Mustad R70 Size 18
Bead – 5/64 nickel bead
Thread – 8/0 black
Rib – Fine silver wire
Note – Many tiers coat the body of the fly with head cement or clear lacquer

Bead Headed Egg

Tied by Bill Willmert

Hook – Eagle Claw 038A Size 10
Bead – 5/32 gold
Weight – 6 wraps .015 lead pushed under bead pinning it in place
Thread – 6/0 red
Body – 2-4 pieces of pink McFly Foam.
Note — One small strand of celrise McFly Foam is tied in with the rest of the McFly Foam to make a hot spot.

Bill Willmert

*Early morning is my favorite.
If you sleep in, you usually
can't pick your water.
You take what's left.*

Bill Willmert was born in Wisconsin in 1949. He started fly fishing in Wisconsin for spring pike in the late 70's. During the summer he switched to smallmouth bass, and in fall, fly fishing for steelhead, salmon and lake run brown trout.

Bill moved to southeast Missouri in the early 90's. There, he fished for largemouth bass, chain pickerel and park trout. There weren't many really big game fish, so he started fishing for rough fish. During this time, he and his wife set several line class tippet IGFA world records. Gar and bowfin were personal favorites. Once while fishing in Texas, Bill hooked an 8-foot alligator and fought it for over an hour thinking it was an alligator gar.

Bill has demonstrated tying some of his patterns at the Sowbug Festival, the FFF Southern Conclave and the FFF International Conclave.

Bill currently lives in Heber Springs with his wife, 11 dogs and a blind cat. He works as a foundry engineer in a local manufacturing facility.

Bill does most of his fishing on the Little Red River. He also guides on the Little Red and does some custom tying as well. His favorite fly fishing is still for northern pike and smallmouth bass, so he spends a few weeks each spring in northern Ontario, fishing Rainy Lake.

Interview:

Q: How long have you trout fished?
A: I fished for lake run brown trout and steel head in Lake Michigan tributaries in the late 70's. I started fishing river trout shortly after I moved to Missouri in 1992.

Q: How long have you fished the Little Red River?
A: I started fly fishing for trout in the Little Red when I moved to Heber Springs in 2000.

Q: What do you do in your non-fishing life?
A: I'm a foundry engineer for St. Jean Industries.

Q: Have you fly fished for other fish than trout?
A: I have caught 57 different species of freshwater fish.

Q: How has this influenced your trout fishing?
A: Fishing for different kinds of fish made me much more versatile by learning to fish different habitats and a variety of flies and leader arrangements. Many of these fish involved long casting, so my casting improved. Best of all, I learned to fight big fish on light tippets.

Q: What do you look for in selecting a piece of water to fish?
A: I like tailouts the best. My next favorite water would be weedy pools. Moving water 2- to 4-feet deep with patches of weeds is normally good streamer water.

Q: Who has influenced your fishing and how?
A: Larry Dahlberg's video on pike fishing got me interested in fly fishing. Rick Hayden in Missouri started me fishing for trout. We also fished quite a bit for rough fish. Royce Dam taught me how to tie flies. Bob Silzer showed me how to actively strip emergers and Rick Rasnick has tried to teach me to midge fish. (Silzer and Rasnick are also featured in this publication.)

Q: Do you primarily wade or boat fish?
A: I do both, but I prefer wading.

Q: Do you use a wading staff?
A: Yes. I use it more getting to the water than I do in the water.

Q: What times of day do you primarily fish?
A: Early morning is my favorite. If you sleep in you usually can't pick your water. You take what's left.

Q: Do you fish high water?
A: Deep, indicator fishing is boring. I try to avoid fishing high water.

Q: What are your favorite flies?
A: Deena
      Misfit
      MEHO Midge
      CDC No Elk
      Yong Special
      Furbug

Q: How do you fish them?
A: Both the Deena and the Misfit are made for stripping. Usually very short and very quick strips work the best. The others are dead drifted. The CDC No Elk can be fished as a dry fly or stripped as an emerger just under the surface.

Q: Does fly color matter?
A: Yes, but it's not the most important trigger. Size and shape make a bigger difference.

Q: Do you use any special leaders or rigs for your favorite flies?
A: I fish the Deena on a sink tip line with a leader of 4- to 6-pound Ande line about 5-feet long. I fish the Misfit on a 12- to 15-foot, 6X leader. If stripping flies on a floating line, it is very important to use the longest leader that you can cast comfortably. I almost always use a 7X, 2- to 3-foot fluorocarbon tippet when I midge fish.

Q: Does your leader change with different flies?
A: I'll usually use either one of the leaders that I mentioned.

Q: Do you use fluorocarbon?
A: Only for tippets.

Q: Do you use strike indicators? What kind?
A: I normally use a small Styrofoam ball with a rubber band core.

Q: What size fly do you fish most often?
A: Deena – Size 8
     Mistfit – Size 16
     Midges – Size 20-22
     CDC No Elk – Size 16-18

Q: What kind of knots do you use?
A: Flyline to Backing – Bimini Twist loop to whipped loop in fly line.
     Fly line to leader – Nail knot
     Leader to Tippet – Double surgeons
     Tippet to Fly – For a Streamer a Duncan Loop
     For the rest, a Double Surgeons loop

Q: What is your favorite piece of equipment?
A: Simm's G3 waders, Spring Creek forceps by Dr. Slick, Folstaff wading staff, and the lanyard that Jamie Rouse's wife, Katie, made. (Rouse is a featured fisherman in this publication.) I also really like my Ketchum Release tool. Releasing fish without taking them out of the water or handling them is important.

Q: What tips or advice would you give a first time fisherman on the Little Red River?
A: Learn to cast well. Avoid repeatedly letting your cast land in front of you and picking it up and recasting. If your cast hits the water, fish it. Letting your line hit the water in front of you over and over spooks a lot of fish. Also, wade quietly. Don't walk into the river splashing all over and then start fishing. Maybe you can cast to your fish without entering the water. If you have to wade in, do it quietly.

Q: What's your favorite rod, reel and line combination?
A: Rod: Sage 10-foot, 4-weight, Z axis rod. This is by far my favorite all-around rod for the Little Red. I use a Ryall 5-6 reel, and a 5-weight, 15-foot, Type III sink tip for streamers, and a 5-weight WF floating line for nymphs and emergers. My favorite streamer rod is a 5-weight, 9-foot TFO, TiCr.

Q: Do you tie your own flies?
A: Yes.

Q: Do you design your own flies?
A: Yes, I usually fish with flies that are my own.

Q: What about bead heads?
A: I use black bead heads the most on midges. In low light or dingy water, I generally use nickel beads. On streamers, I use bead heads when I fish deeper pools or, again, in dingy water.

Q: How do the seasons affect your fishing.
A: Except for fishing deeper pools in the fall for pre-spawn browns, they don't.

Q: Does your fly selection change with water type or seasonally?
A: In late summer and fall I fish a Mistfit more. It's a great brown trout fly.

Q: Does your favorite river access change with the seasons?
A: In the winter I like to fish JFK Park. I fish a few pools around Cow Shoals in the fall and I usually fish less at JFK then. In the fall, I also really like the drift from Lobo to Dripping Springs. In the summer, I'm indifferent. In early spring, I like to fish the lower river because of the caddis hatches.

Q: How does the time of day affect your fishing?
A: I like to fish early in the morning or later in the afternoon the best in the spring, summer and fall. In the winter I like afternoons the best.

Q: Do you prefer rising, falling or stable water?
A: Stable and low, but with a current.

Q: Are fish signs important to your style of fishing?
A: Of course. Rising fish tell you that they are there

Fly Fishing on the Red

and hungry. The rise form can tell you what they are eating.

Q: What is your favorite fishing technique? (Swing, strip or dead drift.)
A: Stripping.

Q: What has been the biggest change you have seen on the Little Red River?
A: I have only fished the Little Red since 2000, but I have noticed a significant increase in fishing pressure since that time.

Q: What changes do you or don't care for?
A: Obviously, I don't like the crowding. Brook trout haven't been stocked since 2007, and I really miss them, and Didymo algae has spread into areas where I didn't see it a few years ago.

Q: Do you ever night fish?
A: I should, but I really don't like night fishing. Night time noises give me the creeps.

CDC No Elk

Originated by Bill Willmert
Tied by Bill Willmert

Hook – Mustad R70 Size 16
Thread – 8/0 black
Note – The body, legs and wing are all tied from the same CDC feather. The entire fly is made from a single CDC feather, either a type one or type four CDC feather.
Body – Twisted CDC feather palmered
Legs – CDC feather, the legs are formed by the part of the feather that is not trapped against the hook forming the body.
Wing – The portion of the CDC feather that is left over. Trap the fibers that are left in a loop of thread, and snug them to the top of the hook shank.
Note – A good way to learn to tie this fly is to tie a CDC & Elk and omit the Deer hair wing. Instead trap some fibers from the portion of CDC feather that is left and tie them to the top of the hook.

Deena

Originated by Bill Willmert
Tied by Bill Willmert

Hook – Mustad 9672 Size 8
Thread – 8/0 olive
Weight – 12 to 24 wraps of .020" lead wire
Tail – Tip of a olive marabou blood feather. Note - Pull out the tip of the feather and include part of the stem in the tail to reduce trapping the tail under the hook bend while fishing.
Body –Olive Uni-Mohair
Flash – Two strands of olive dyed pearl Flashabou
Collar – Olive mallard flank feather wrapped as a soft hackle
Head – Tying thread

MEHO Midge

Originated by Bill Willmert
Tied by Bill Willmert

Hook – Tiemco 100 Size 20 to 24
Bead – 1/16" Nickel or black bead
Thread – 8/0 white
Body – 2-4 fibers of Super Hair
Thorax – Super hair used for the body is whip finished behind the bead to form wing case. (Note: Blue and white were selected to illustrate the fly for this photograph. Bill's favorite combination of Super Hair is two strands of brown and one strand of black with a black Cyclops head.)

Misfit Midge

Originated by Bill Willmert
Tied by Bill Willmert

Hook – R70 Size 16
Thread – 8/0 olive
Rib – Micro Larve Lace
Hackle – Brown rooster saddle stripped on one side and palmered to the head
Body – Olive dyed pearl Flashabou
Head – 8/0 black thread.

Bibliography

Barr, John, Barr Flies, Mechanicsburg, PA, Stackpole Books, 2007

Best, A. K., A. K.'s Fly Box, New York, NY, Lyons and Burford Publishers, 1996

Best, A. K., Advanced Fly Tying, Guilford, CN, The Lyons Press, 2001

Best, A. K., Production Fly Tying, Boulder, CO, Pruett Publishing Company, 1989

Borger, Gary, Presentation, Wausau, WI, Tomorrow River Press, 1995

Borger, Gary, Designing Trout Flies, Wausau, WI, Tomorrow River Press, 1991

Borger, Gary, Naturals, A Guide to Food Organisms of the Trout, Harrisburg, PA, Stackpole Books, 1980

Borger, Gary, Nymphing, Harrisburg, PA, Stackpole Books, 1979

Camera, Phil, Fly Tying with Synthetics, New York, NY, Voyageur Press, 1992

Caucci, Al, Nastasi, Bob, Hatches II, New York, NY, Lyons and Burford Publishers, 1975

Craven, Charlie, Basic Fly Tying, New Cumberland, PA, Headwater Books, 2008

Dam, Royce, The Practical Fly Tier, Mechanicsburg, PA, Stackpole Books, 2002

Dennis, Jack, Tying Flies with Jack and Friends, Jackson Hole, WY, Snake River Books, 1993

Dennis, Jack, Western Trout Fly Tying Manual, Jackson Hole, WY, Snake River Books, 1991

Dennis, Jack, Western Trout Fly Tying Manual, Vol. II, Jackson Hole, WY, Snake River Books, 1995

Dorsey, Pat, Fly Fishing Tail Waters, Mechanicsburg, PA, Stackpole Books, 2009

Edwards, Oliver, Flytyers Masterclass, Wayne, NJ, Stoeger Publishing Company, 1999

Engle, Ed, Fishing Small Flies, Mechanicsburg, PA, Stackpole Books, 2005

Engle, Ed, Fly Fishing the Tailwaters, Harrisburg, PA, Stackpole Books, 1991

Engle, Ed, Tying Small Flies, Mechanicsburg, PA, Stackpole Books, 2004

Flick, Art, New Streamside Guide, New York, NY, Lyons and Burford Publishers, 1969

Fogg, Rodger, The Art of the Wet Fly, London, England, A&C Black Ltd, 1978

Gierach, John, Good Flies, New York, NY, Lyon's Press, 2000

Hafele, Rick, Nymph Fishing Rivers & Streams, Mechanicsburg, PA, Stackpole Books, 2006

Hicks, Danny, Ozarks Blue-Ribbon Trout Streams, Portland, Oregon, Frank Amato Publications, 2002

Hidy, Vernon, Sports Illustrated Wet Fly Fishing, Philadelphia and New York, J. B. Lippincott Company, 1961

Holbrook, Don, Koch, Ed, Midge Magic, Mechanicsburg, PA, Stackpole Books, 2001

Hughes, Dave, Essential Trout Flies, Mechanicsburg, PA, Stackpole Books, 2000

Hughes, Dave, Fishing the Four Seasons, Guilford, CT, The Lyon's Press, Imprint of The Globe Pequot Press,

Hughes, Dave, Nymph Fishing, Portland, OR, Frank Amato Publications, 1995

Hughes, Dave, Nymphs for Streams and Stillwaters, Mechanicsburg, PA, Stackpole Books, 2009

Hughes, Dave, Reading the Water, Mechanicsburg, PA, 1998

Hughes, Dave, Trout Flies, Mechanicsburg, PA, Stackpole Books, 1999

Hughes, Dave, Wet Flys, Mechanicsburg, PA, Stackpole Books, 1995

Iwamasa, Ken, Iwamasa Flies, Boulder, CO, Pruett Publishing Company, 1989

John Goddard, A Fly Fisher's Reflections, Guiltford, CT, Lyons Press, 2002

Johnson, Paul C., The Scientific Angler, New York, NY, Charles Scribner's Sons, 1984

Judy, John, Slack Line Strategies for Fly Fishing, Mechanicsburg, PA, Stackpole Books, 1994

Kaufmann, Randall, Fly Patterns of Umpqua Feather Merchants, Glide, OR, Umpqua Feather Merchants, 1995

Kaufmann, Randall, Kaufmann, Mary, Fly Patterns, Moose, WY, Western Fisherman's Press, 2008

Kaufmann, Randall, Nymph Fly Tying Manual, Portland, OR, Frank Amato Publications, 1975

Kaufmann, Randall, The Fly Tyers Nymph Manual, Portland, OR, Western Fisherman's Press, 1992

Kaufmann, Randall, Tying Nymphs, Portland, Oregon, Western Fisherman's Press, 1994

Kite, Oliver, Nymph Fishing in Practice, Shrewsberry, England, Swan Hill Press, 2000

Kreh, Lefty, Practical Fishing Knots II, New York, NY, Lyons and Burford Publishers, 1991

Krivanec, Karel, Czech Nymph, Czech Republic, Grayling & Trout Publishing, 2007

LaFontaine, Gary, Caddis Flies, New York, NY, Lyons and Burford Publishers, 1981

LaFontaine, Gary, The Dry Fly, New Angles, Helena, MT, Greycliff Publishing, 1990

LaFontaine, Gary, Trout Flies, Proven Patterns, Helena, MT, Greycliff Publishing Co., 1993

Lawton, Terry, Nymph Fishing, A History of the Art and Practice, Mechanicsburg, PA, Stackpole Books, 2005

Leeson, Ted, Schollmeyer, Jim, The Fly Tier's Benchside Reference, Portland, OR, Frank Amato Publications, 1998

Leisenring, James E., Hidy, Vernon, The Art of Tying the Net, Fly and Fishing the Flymph, New York, NY, Crown Publishers, 1971

Links, Leon, Tying Flies with CDC, Mechanicsburg, PA, Stackpole Books, 2002

Lisenman, Bob, Galloup, Kelly, Modern Streamers for Trophy Trout, Woodstock, VT, The Countryman's Press, 1999

Marinaro, Vincent, In the Ring of the Rise, New York, NY, Crown Publishers, 1996

Martin, Darrel, Fly Tying Methods, New York, NY, Lyons and Burford Publishers, 1987

Martin, Darrel, Micropatterns, Tying and Fishing the Small Fly, New York, NY, Lyons and Burford Publishers, 1994

McGee, Allen, Tying and Fishing Soft Hadded Nymphs, Portland, OR, Frank Amato Publishers, 2007

Meck, Charles, How to Catch More Trout, Greenville, PA, Beaver Pond Publishing, 2001

Meck, Charles, The Hatches Made Simple, Woodstock, VT, The Countryman's Press, 2002

Mercer, Mike, Creative Fly Tying, Mill Creek, WA, Wild River Press, 2005

Mid South Fly Fishers, Home Waters, Memphis, TN, Impressions Ink, 1997

Migel, Michael, Wright, Leonard, The Master's on the Nymph, Garden City, NY, Nick Lyons Books, 1979

Morris, Skip, Trout Flies for Rivers, Mechanics, PA, Stackpole Books, 2009

Nemes, Sylvester, Soft-Hackled Fly Imitations, Bozeman, MT, Published by Author, 1991

Nemes, Sylvester, The Soft-Hackled Fly Addict, Mechanicsburg, PA, Stackpole Books, 1993

Nemes, Sylvester, The Soft-Hackled Fly, Old Greenwich, CN, Self Published by Author, 1975

Nemes, Sylvester, Two Centuries of Soft-Hackled Flies, Mechanicsburg, PA, Stackpole Books, 2004

Polly, Rosborough, Tying and Fishing the Fuzzy Nymphs, Harrisburg, PA, Stackpole Books, 1988

Proper, Datus, What the Trout Said, New York, NY, Nick Lyons Books, 1989

Rosenbauer, Tom, Reading Trout Streams, New York, NY, Lyons and Burford Publishers, 1988

Sanchez, Scott, A New Generation of Trout Flies, Mill Creek, WA, Wild River Press, 2005

Sawda, Ken, Wet Flys: 400 Patterns and Dressing Techniques, Toyko, Japan, Tulcan Books, 1995

Sawyer, Frank, Nymphs and the Trout, New York, NY, Crown Publishers, 1970

Scheck, Art, Tying Better Flies, Woodstock, VT, The Countryman Press, 2003

Schollmeyer, Jim, Leeson, Ted, Tying Emergers, Portland, OR, Frank Amato Publishing, 2004

Schwiebert, Ernest, Nymphs, New York, NY, Winchester Press, 1973

Shenk, Ed, Fly Rod Trouting, Harrisburg, PA, Stackpole Books, 1989

Soucie, Gary, Woolly Wisdom, Portland, OR, Frank Amato Publications, 2005

Stalcup, Shane, Mayflies "Top to Bottom", Portland, OR, Frank Amato Publications, 2002

Steeves III, Harrison R., Tying Flies with Foam, Fur and Feathers, Mechanicsburg, PA, Stackpole Books, 2003

Stetzer, Randle, Scott, Flies: The Best One Thousand, Portland, OR, Frank Amato Publications, 1992

Stewart, Dick, Allen, Farrow, Flies for Trout, North Conway, NH, Mountain Pond Publishing, 1993

Swisher, Doug, Richards, Carl, Selective Trout, New York, NY, Nick Lyons Books, 1971

Takahashi, Rick, Hubka, Jerry, Modern Midges, New Cumberland, PA, Headwater Books, 2009

Whitlock, Dave, A Guide to Aquatic Trout Food, New York, NY, Lyons and Burford Publishers, 1982

Wright, Leonard M. Jr., The Ways of the Trout, New York, NY, Lyons and Burford Publishers, 1985

Wright, Steve, Ozark Trout Tales, Fayetteville, AR, White River Chronicle, 1995

Wulff, Lee, Wulff on Flies, Harrisburg, PA, Stackpole Books, 1985

Wyatt, Bob, Trout Hunting, Mechanicsburg, PA, Stackpole Books, 2005

About the Author

Bill Willmert was born in 1949. He graduated from the University of Wisconsin, Milwaukee, in 1973.

Bill started fly fishing for pike and salmon in the 70's and has since fished all over the United States in fresh and salt water. He has set 26 IGFA fly rod records. He started fishing for rough fish while living in southwest Missouri. During this time, he and his wife also set several line class tippet IGFA world records. Gar and bowfin were personal favorites.

Bill now does most of his fishing on the Little Red River where he also guides and does some custom tying as well. His favorite fly fishing is still for northern pike and smallmouth bass, so he spends a few weeks each spring in northern Ontario, fishing

Bill has demonstrated tying some of his patterns at the Sowbug Festival, The FFF Southern Conclave and the FFF International Conclave.

NOTES

NOTES

Made in the USA
San Bernardino, CA
28 October 2015